# GET IT
*together*

# GET IT

## together

### DITCH THE CHAOS,
### DO THE WORK,
### AND DESIGN
### *Your Success*

# LAUREN BERGER

Mc
Graw
Hill
Education

New York   Chicago   San Francisco   Athens   London   Madrid
Mexico City   Milan   New Delhi   Singapore   Sydney   Toronto

1 2 3 4 5 6 QVS 22 21 20 19 18

ISBN 978-1-260-14295-2
MHID 1-260-14295-7

e-ISBN 978-1-260-14296-9
e-MHID 1-260-14296-5


**Library of Congress Cataloging-in-Publication Data**

Names: Berger, Lauren (Lauren E.) author.
Title: Get it together : ditch the chaos, do the work, and design your success / Lauren Berger.
Description: 1 Edition. | New York : McGraw-Hill Education, 2018.
Identifiers: LCCN 2018030687| ISBN 9781260142952 (paperback) | ISBN 1260142957
Subjects: LCSH: Success. | Success in business. | Motivation (Psychology)
Classification: LCC BF637.S8 B4657 2018 | DDC 158.1--dc23 LC record available at https://lccn.loc.gov/2018030687


McGraw-Hill Education books are available at special quantity discounts to use as premiums and sales promotions or for use in corporate training programs. To contact a representative, please visit the Contact Us pages at www.mhprofessional.com.

*My third book is dedicated to my parents, Ira and Sherry Berger, who've helped me get it together and keep it together since day one. And when things aren't together, they are the first to let me know. I love you, Mom and Dad.*

# CONTENTS

# CONTENTS

# INTRODUCTION

"Jab, Cross, Hook, Uppercut! Jab, Cross, Hook, Uppercut!" My trainer yelled out boxing moves. He was loud for the sake of being loud. I followed his commands as best I could with my big pink gloves. I felt like Gigi Hadid whenever I practiced with him. "Eye contact, stop yawning, put your shoulder into it, use more energy, stop yawning. . . ." I could tell he was starting to get frustrated with my lackluster performance. I didn't mind; I was relieved to not be in charge for the first time all day. I meant to go straight to the gym from my office, but, as usual, I forgot my gym bag. Our session started at 5 p.m. and I had rolled in around 5:20. I was known as the "late client."

My brain was still in a million pieces from the hustle and bustle of the day. The highlight reel? My team didn't hit their sales goals, my assistant put in her two weeks' notice, I still have several follow-up e-mails to send, I need to call my mom back, and my closest friends are in a group text message fight that is making my phone ding nonstop. If all of that wasn't enough, I felt a case of the sniffles coming on, and the trainer was right . . . I was tired!

Boom, boom, boom . . . my glove would meet his boxing pads. I boxed in leggings and an oversized gray hoodie that probably needed to be retired years ago. They say that when you *look* the part, you *feel* the part. I certainly wasn't feeling the part in my sad hoodie. The trainer looked at me and rolled his eyes, "Wearing your dad's clothes again?" I smirked back at him, ignoring his comment. I tried to keep my focus, but the trainer could tell I was distracted. My mind was everywhere except at the gym.

"You need to work on this, Lauren, seriously. You seem to be all over the place. I want to see constant improvement, none of this laziness. You need to *get it together!*" Wow! A harsh claim from the trainer at my gym, whom I'd only met one month ago. But in all honesty . . . he was right.

Welcome to my third book. I'm so excited to take you on this personal journey and show you how I've been able to "get it together." I started the writing process feeling frustrated with life and work. I was going nonstop but not seeing the results I wanted. I felt like a hot mess, like I was all over the place, and I agreed with my trainer, I needed to get it together. Today, after grueling hard work, focus, and the longing to change, I can tell you, my life is more together than I thought it would be.

## WHAT YOU WILL LEARN IN THIS BOOK

You may know me from my other two books, *All Work, No Pay* and *Welcome to the Real World*. In those books, I wrote about the power of internships and career opportunities, and how navigating those experiences properly can help you get from where you are to where you want to be. This new title is the perfect follow-up to those books.

In *Get It Together*, I take my advice one step further and help you create your ultimate path to success. Like my other books, *Get It Together* is rooted in the workplace but provides you with actionable steps that you can utilize at home as well. As the reader, you will walk away from this book armed with techniques and tips to quickly integrate into your daily routine to make you feel more together.

We kick off the book with some solutions for success in **Chapter 1**. The reoccurring themes I pull out here are brought up repeatedly throughout the book. I can't stress enough the importance of these principles as they guide the rest of the book's material and are mantras that I try to live by.

In **Chapter 2**, I'll introduce you to my daily routine (think: day in the life) and encourage you to think about reinventing your own schedule. A daily routine is our opportunity to execute and accomplish our goals, so it's important we take that seriously. And the best part? Every day is a blank slate to start over and lock that routine into place!

**Chapter 3** is about learning how to cope with failure. One clear lesson that I learned in trying to get my life together was that failure and rejection happen. And when it comes, it comes in hard. In this chapter, I help you handle these issues and find strategies to better manage both failure and rejection. Knowing how to do this will help you ultimately get it together.

**Chapter 4** focuses on goal-setting, productivity, organization, and leaving work feeling satisfied. In this chapter, I discuss time and how to best track and plan how your time is spent. The exercise in this chapter (YQMB—stay tuned to find out what this stands for!) will help you to not only create goals, but learn to create Action Plans too.

**Chapter 5** covers everything you need to be successful at work (all of your tools) including your calendar, inbox, bullet journal, and project management system. I go through each tool and discuss best practices based on how I stay organized at work.

**Chapter 6** is all about efficiency at work and saving time while performing at a high level. In this chapter, I cover how to do great work. I'll cover how to focus, prioritize, run efficient meetings, become more results-oriented, network internally and externally, and so much more.

**Chapter 7** dives into the idea that although social networks allow us to brand ourselves and connect with more people than we ever thought possible, it also adds 100 more things to our to-do lists and is one of the biggest distractions we face. This chapter will help you evaluate which networks to use, how to use them, how to manage the noise on all your networks, and even how to really disconnect.

**Chapter 8** is our professional and personal relationships chapter. Since our colleagues, supervisors, friends, and family are whom we spend the most time with, it's important to learn the best ways to manage these relationships. Here we will define the professional and personal relationships we have and how to best handle them. I discuss strategies for dealing with conflict at work and in your personal life. As someone who is from Florida and now lives across the country in California, I share my own tips on staying connected with loved ones no matter how far apart you are.

**Chapter 9** covers tips for the mind, body, and soul. I cover fitness, eating healthy, sleep, and most important—relaxation techniques. As an added bonus, I list 40 great ways that you can relax—starting today. This chapter is important because it's *not* about work and only about *you*.

As you read these next chapters and start to create your own personal plan to get it together, #GIT, please keep me posted on your progress. I'm super accessible, and thanks to social media, we can be in touch throughout your journey.

Please feel free to message me, tweet me, DM me—anything you want. I'm @InternQueen on every social platform! I'm genuinely interested in hearing the story of how each one of you is working to get it together.

And now, without further ado, I ask you to join me in this adventure of self-improvement, professional development, business savvy, and personal wellness. Let's get our lives together @InternQueen—#GIT!

## HOW THIS BOOK CAME TO BE

Before we dive into the first chapter, I want to tell you how this book came to be and why I'm so excited for the personal journey we're about to take together.

When you pull back the curtain, you'll find this book has been a work in progress for some time. In fact, the first version of this project (with a different title and take) was put together almost three years ago. Originally, I wanted to write a book about the word *busy*. I felt that it had crept up and invaded our lives in a way we couldn't handle.

I couldn't escape the busy. Every work call or personal call started with the person on the other line telling me how busy he or she was—disguising the word with silly phrases like "I'm running around like a chicken with my head cut off," "I'm slammed," "I'm spent," "I'm crazed." I felt that "busy" was used as an excuse. People couldn't see me, meet with me, or even talk to me because of how busy they were. I also felt that the word *busy* wrongfully became interchangeable with the word *successful*. Whoever was the busiest was also the most important. I didn't like the busy competition. It left me feeling like I wasn't good enough because I wasn't as busy as everyone else. Or perhaps I was just as busy but didn't talk about it (or boast about it) in the way everyone else did. As a result, I started to subconsciously try to add random tasks and events to my calendar just to feel busy and accepted. This left me feeling overwhelmed, confused, and feeling like I'd lost myself somewhere under all of those forced plans and activities.

I was passionate about the *Busy* project but couldn't seem to find an angle that made sense. Publishers pushed me to be more academic in tone, but it just felt forced—the book no longer felt like my own voice. Long story short, the concept wasn't working and needed to be modified. I desperately wanted to provide my readers with value, not just an idea, but tangible tips that they could put into action immediately, actions that would create meaningful change. I immediately got to work with this new idea in mind and was amazed at

## Thanks so much for being a great GG Leader!

This is a special gift from us to say thank you for all the wonderful work you have done so far leading your chapter. We hope you enjoy it! Our favorite chapter is the one on goal setting. We hope it inspires you to set a goal like earning the Intergenerational Service Award so you can request a recommendation letter from us.

♡ *GG National*

how often I'd hear people in everyday life say some variation of "I just need to get it together!" I began to research this idea more and discovered a December 2015 Gallop poll that revealed "61 percent of working Americans said they did not have enough time to do the things they wanted to do."[1] I knew I was onto something special. When I started writing about this new concept, I kept it exclusive to the workplace and how to get your work life together. But I quickly realized that my work life intersected with every other part of my life: family, friends, free time, my house, my personal fitness goals . . . everything. Getting it together wasn't just a workplace goal, it was an everyplace goal.

In addition to feeling *busy*, why else did we all feel so distracted, disconnected, and "not together"? Ironically, social media (the tool that is supposed to connect us) seems to have played quite the role in creating (or at least enhancing) the chaotic world we're all living in. And think about the pressure that we put on ourselves to uphold our Instagram-worthy lifestyles—it's insane! We can't live up to the impossible standards we set. We want to be the best worker, friend, parent, sibling, colleague—the list goes on and on. Not only do we want to act like we have it all together and go through the motions of having it all together, but we also want to look like we have it all together. We want to wear the cutest outfits while doing our work, seeing the world, and making things happen. Meanwhile, the more we try to be everything to everyone, the more we find ourselves constantly falling short of our own expectations and accomplishing nothing. As Erin Falconer says so candidly in her book, *How to Get Sh*t Done*, "nobody cares that you can do it all."[2]

We can't be perfect as perfect doesn't exist. What we can do is reframe our thinking and strive to be better, more strategic, more prepared. The moment we focus on perfection, we immediately lose. We give ourselves anxiety, stress, migraines, gray hair, and breakouts. The American Psychological Association reports that 39 percent of millennials say their stress has increased in the last year.[3] And it makes sense because we create our own stress. We spend our time diligently adding items to our to-do lists, commitments to our calendar, and heavily filtered photos to social media. Worst of all, we want to keep this stress a secret from our friends, family, and especially ourselves. We don't want to admit that we don't have it all under control. We desperately want everyone to think we have it all together, when it often feels like the furthest thing from the truth. We are so tangled up in our lives that we can't see how to simplify them. And the truth? It doesn't have to be this complicated.

I want you to be able to take your time with this book. It is filled with lifestyle changes and small tips that can really go a long way. If you rush the read, you won't be able to push yourself and really start implementing my advice. Please, go slow, read one chapter at a time, and really consider the information I'm sharing. I know that everyone has different days, different schedules, different obstacles, different strengths and weaknesses—but I'm confident that you can find something in this book that speaks to you.

Getting it together isn't easy. If it was, you wouldn't have picked up this title in the first place. But I promise, we'll fight through it together and we won't stop until we feel better, lighter, and more in-place.

# INTERVIEWS

In addition to my own advice, I wanted to get different experts to weigh in on how they manage their lives at work and at home. As soon as each interview started, it reaffirmed my interest and belief in the importance of this topic; I couldn't believe how much we all had in common, regardless of our jobs. We were all fighting the same battle and had the same resources to achieve our goals. Each interview taught me new techniques that I could use in trying to get it together. At times, I was selfish with my interview questions, asking questions that I needed to hear the answers to. And I'm confident that you and I have things in common, and you'll also enjoying hearing the answers to my questions.

To determine whose interviews would be the best fit for the book, I first went to our audience and asked whom they wanted to hear from. From that brainstorming session, I was able to secure interviews with business experts, social media influencers, and more!

I was lucky enough to get to interview **Laura Vanderkam**, one of the most popular authors on the planet when it comes to time management, for the book. She's written several books on the subject including her latest title, *Off the Clock: Feel Less Busy While Getting More Done*. She also happens to be one of my favorite authors as I always learn so much by reading her books. **Sarah Boyd** is the founder of Simply, the larger-than-life and worldwide fashion/beauty/women empowerment conference,[4] and president of West Coast operations for Nylon, its new parent company. I've known Sarah since before she started her megabrand, and she's always been a force to be reckoned with. Her brand receives a ton of celebrity attention from people like Olivia Culpo, Catt Sadler, and more. Another out-of-this-world entrepreneur that I spoke with for this book is MissionU cofounder **Adam Braun**. You may remember Braun from his previous nonprofit that he founded, Pencils of Promise. Adam is author of *The Promise of a Pencil: How an Ordinary Person Can Create Extraordinary Change* and, of course, the brother of music superhero Scooter Braun. In his new venture, MissionU, Braun is disrupting the education space with an alternative to a traditional four-year college.

I also wanted to speak to the most organized person on the planet, and luckily, I knew exactly whom to call. **Jen Robin**, CEO of Life in Jeneral, a company that gets hired to go into people's homes and work spaces to clean them up and get them organized. You'll have to start following Jen's Instagram feed, @LifeInJeneral, and you'll also be inspired to get it together. And finally, you'll hear from one of my closest friends, **Rachel Doyle**, the CEO and Founder of Glamour-Gals (glamourgals.org), a nonprofit that she's been running for over 18 years that connects young women with the elderly through makeovers and companionship. Rachel and I run businesses of a similar size and are always leaning on each other for advice and talking about how we can both get it together!

I was so excited to also include interviews with social media influencers like **Ashley Robertson** (www.theteacherdiva .com) and **Lauryn Hock** (www.lauryncakes.com). They both have the type of Instagram feeds that others dream about! They always look put together and somehow keep up with a demanding schedule, major content pushes, constant sponsorship deals, and insane engagement from followers. I also interviewed one of my favorite YouTubers (and our network's favorite), **Brooke Miccio** (@BrookeMiccio), who has a huge following on both Instagram and YouTube and somehow runs her own business, grows her personal brand, pumps out content, and is a full-time student at the University of Georgia.

• • •

We all have that person in our lives who seems to know everything about time management. For me, that person is **Josh Notes**, a friend and an executive efficiency and renewable energy systems expert. He provides great advice throughout the book on doing great work. When I interviewed Josh Notes, he said something that stuck with me. He asked me a trick question: "What's the one thing that we all have in common with one another, regardless of how special or important someone might be?" I had no idea. "Time!" he declared. "We all have the exact same amount of time—168 hours in a week to do whatever we want with." And Josh is right. We are all playing with the same tools, and when you remind yourself of that, it sort of evens the playing field.

## WHAT'S NEXT?

If we actually "got our lives together," what would we do with this newfound success? People have always told me that I have great potential, but that I always tend to get in my own way. Whether it was not completing tasks, not getting to bed on time, being messy, or ignoring priorities on my to-do list, I was sometimes my biggest issue. But if I could simply do all of those things properly, what would I discover about myself? If we weren't constantly feeling that we are buried under messy piles of dirty clothes, dishes in the sink, empty iced coffee cups, and purses filled with scrap paper, can you imagine what we would be capable of?

I'm here to help you discover exactly that. Let's see what your life could be like if you were able to remove the busy, the expectations of others, and just focus on what you truly want.

If you're thinking to yourself, "OK, well, this sounds nice, but how long will it take to 'Get It Together'?"—I totally get it. It's a fair question.

For me, it was challenging. My eyes were bigger than my stomach. I thought I could change everything about my lifestyle all at once. I soon learned that habits are powerful behaviors to break or change. So, in order to reset my lifestyle, I first had to recognize all of the things I was doing that were holding me back.

Every night, I'd write about what was working and not working in my life, and then I'd write down what I was going to do to fix those problems I was experiencing. Today, four months later, I can tell you with great confidence that I've experienced change—and great change at that! I'm in tune with my own needs and therefore can make decisions that are the best for me regardless of what others think. My decisions also feel intentional and not random. On a daily basis I'm aware of what I need to do and I am able to focus and create my own "distraction free" zone, regardless of where I am. I've also found that I enjoy leaving my phone at home or on the other side of the room for long periods of time. These changes have not only been beneficial to me, but I'm now able to help others by sharing the tips that have worked in my life as well.

Just yesterday, a friend called and started venting about her problems, but instead of joining her pity party, I simply said, "Here's all you need to do. Evaluate the way you spend your time at work and focus on getting more work done during the workday. I know you're busy, but try to really focus on your projects. Don't sit on your e-mail all day long." (Easier said than done, I know.)

Every day I remind myself of the guiding principles in this book. They help me to recognize my own suboptimal behaviors and fully understand how to navigate difficult situations. The best thing about these principles is that we already have the tools. We internally possess the skills—we just need to remind ourselves to activate them in times of need.

**So, let's do this—let's get it together!**

# *Chapter* 1

## I NEED TO GET
## IT TOGETHER

In Chapter 1, we will review the 17 guiding principles of the book that are crucial to your success. These principles include loving yourself, knowing your needs and priorities, preparing for everything, celebrating you, creating boundaries, valuing your time, and so much more.

## OUR GUIDING PRINCIPLES

To make sure this book reflected real life, I journaled about the daily actions I was taking to get it together and the effect they had. This process brought to light the root causes of the issues I was having. The following pages capture the solutions that I devised to help frame the material for this book. Think of these solutions as the guiding principles for the book.

## 1. Like Bieber Says, "Love Yourself"

Lately, I'm a big fan of Demi Lovato (and of course, Bieber too!). In fact, I'm such a sucker that I paid for YouTube's Red service just to watch her documentary. Demi talks about self-love a lot in her documentary and throughout her work. After I watched the documentary, I came to realize how big a role self-love should be playing in our lives. Why was I fighting with myself constantly, and feeling like I wasn't good enough? We hold ourselves to ridiculous standards, trying to live our life as if it's being captured for our Instagram Story feeds. Real life happens, and we don't have an edit button or a cool new filter to hide the reality. When you put too much pressure on yourself, apply a gentle reminder—love yourself. Remind yourself of how loved you are throughout this process, and you'll be amazed at how much it can calm you down and center you during tough times.

## 2. Create Healthy Boundaries

A topic that comes up several times throughout the book is boundaries. Before I wrote this book, I didn't incorporate many boundaries into my life. Honestly, I didn't realize what a big problem this was for me. I would literally jump anytime a friend called, texted, asked to make plans, or wanted to travel to or with me. Every time I would just say yes. When I made these instant decisions, I wouldn't consider myself or my desires, I'd just say yes. It didn't matter if I had the time—I'd make time.

Ironically, trying so hard to please other people backfired. Because I was terrible at creating boundaries, I would overcommit and then have to backpedal to get out of the plans I'd made. And even when I wasn't making other people upset, I'd be upsetting myself. I would commit to things, and then realize that I wanted nothing to do with those activities, then I'd question why I said yes in the first place. I didn't feel in control of the way I was spending my time.

Since starting this project, I've slowly implemented healthy boundaries in my work and personal life. Just because someone wants to have a "feelings talk" in the office doesn't mean I pick up the phone and call the person at that very moment. Just because someone else wants to do something on a specific day doesn't mean that I can always make it work. In fact, just the other day I got an e-mail from a team member who asked if I could speak over the weekend. The old Lauren would have immediately written him back and said, "Sure! Call me whenever." But, because I had previously set aside time to work on a project on Saturday, the new Lauren said, "I'm working on a project Saturday, but happy to set aside time to speak on Sunday." For some, that may not seem like a big deal, but for me, this was huge. It not only helped me complete my work on time, but it also helped me to create a small but healthy boundary. Healthy boundaries are needed with friends and family, at work, and even with your social media.

## 3. Cope with Failure—It's Inevitable

The truth is, we don't always get it right. As I've tried to get it together throughout this process, I've experienced a lot of failure and rejection—and it sucks. I can't begin to describe how many mornings I woke up frustrated with myself for not accomplishing a goal or went to sleep knowing that I could have done a better job that day. Since getting it together, though, I've recognized that each day is a step in the process and one that I will eventually learn from.

Failure is life's most important lesson, and once we decide to flip our lives upside down and push ourselves to make a personal change, we will experience a lot of trial and error. You must also be ready to deal with those errors, otherwise you'll fall victim to a ton of self-hate, and it's not healthy for you or the people around you. If you're feeling down on yourself, throughout this process, make sure to keep turning back to the failure and coping section in Chapter 3 of this book. It will help you tremendously. Remember, keep failing until you get it right!

## 4. Of All the People That You Count on, You Should Be Number One

Throughout the process of trying to get it together, I realized how I was constantly in my own way. At night, I'd make an ambitious plan to work out at 6:30 in the morning the next day. The next morning, I'd wake up grumpy and pound my phone alarm until it went silent. I'd go back to sleep thinking, "Ugh, I need sleep. I'm not going to the gym." Later, I'd wake up angry at myself for not following through on my own plan. It was a vicious cycle.

I kept feeling like one side of my brain would plan with the goal of bettering myself (Good Lauren) and then the other side of me would come along and ruin the plan (Bad Lauren). I needed to fix this issue and start making commitments I could stick to, avoid overpromising things to myself, and follow through on my own promises.

Another really helpful way to think about this is to shift your mindset. Think about this. When it comes to making plans with friends, I always keep my word, almost to a fault. Even if going to a specific restaurant or spending time a certain way is the last thing I want to do, I'll likely do it for a friend.

Think about that.

I keep my word and follow through on commitments to friends (that I don't even want to do), and yet I won't do the same for myself! Doesn't that sound ridiculous?

So, next time you try to break your own plans, think of yourself as a friend. Would you do this to a friend? The answer will likely be no.

## 5. You Advocate for You

While my last point was about keeping commitments, this point is about taking yourself seriously. After all, if you aren't going to be your own advocate, who will?

I could go into work tomorrow and spend the entire day doing things for other people. I could answer their questions, chat about their feelings, answer 100-plus e-mails, take all kinds of phone calls, mentor team members, and offer advice to others all day. If that were the case, I'd leave the office having done a lot of stuff but having done nothing for myself. If you don't start every day by reminding yourself of your own goals and actually planning the time for you to work on achieving those goals, you'll never get from where you are to where you want to be. Life is full of requests, questions, demands, phone calls, text messages, and more. If you don't take control, stop the noise, and focus on yourself, who will?

## 6. Determine Your Goals

If you would have asked me about my goals before this book, I would have rattled off 100 different things—well, *if* I could even remember what they were. Today, I understand the importance of focusing on three main goals and being able to recite them anytime and anywhere. I was embarrassed the other day when my book agent asked if I had any New Year's resolutions and I sort of mumbled an answer. The truth was that I *did* have goals, but I couldn't remember what they were. If I don't know my goals—who would? Know your goals, memorize them, and shout them from the rooftops.

In this book, goal-setting will come up a few different times. In Chapter 4, I have a whole exercise for you that helps you create your big goals for the year and come up with Action Plans on how to reach them. Make sure that these goals are clearly thought through each time so you have a better chance at achieving them!

## 7. Know Your Priorities

Everyone has their own priorities. Sometimes we think we have certain priorities, and then something happens and this shifts. I could say that my priority is work until I'm blue in the face, but the reality is—it's not. For me, it's my family: my husband, parents, siblings, extended family, and friends. I would do anything for them. Understanding your priorities and other people's priorities (and accepting that usually they aren't the same) will help you throughout your life (and throughout this book).

In addition to knowing your priorities, you must be able to actually prioritize—at work, at home, and even at the gym. Until recently, I thought I was good at prioritizing. Over time, I've learned this is actually a weakness for me. I'm one of those "everything's important" types. In Chapter 6, I dig into your priorities and really encourage you to think about not only how you can identify your priorities but also how you can better tackle your priorities throughout work and life.

## 8. Know Your Needs

Throughout this process, I was challenged to continue learning about myself. I was constantly asking myself questions: "What makes me happy/sad/mad/upset? How can I be the most productive at work? What can I do to self-motivate? How long do I need to sleep every night in order to feel ready for the next day? How many hours do I need after work before I feel ready for bed?"

By answering these questions and countless more, you will learn to pay close attention to your personal needs throughout this adventure. That knowledge will be power when getting it together.

## 9. Aim for Completion—No Half Tasks

I'm the queen of half-finishing projects and getting road-blocked. Here's an example. In December one of our best sales team members, Katheryn, asked me for business cards. I was excited to use our big credit to Moo.com and get these for her. But every time I'd go to the website to try to finish the project, I'd get an error message upon checkout. I tried multiple times and had no luck. Instead of calling the company or figuring out how to handle the situation, I'd just stop. Months later, Katheryn still didn't have business cards and was starting to get frustrated. And she was right! I kept getting roadblocked and didn't make the time to sit down and get it done. Finally, as I wrote this manuscript, I realized that I need to stop half-completing tasks and get shit done! I blocked a half hour of time on my calendar, called the company, had them walk me through the website, and ordered the business cards. Now, I only wish I'd done that months before.

What I want to reiterate here is that half-completed tasks aren't acceptable, and you have to hold yourself to that standard. I should have made myself complete that task months ago. Make the time to stop what you are doing, figure things out, and check things off your list.

## 10. Embrace Boredom

My college boyfriend once said, "Boredom is the enemy." He said that we should never talk about being bored because there are so many great things to do in life. Because of this, I was convinced for years that boredom was a bad word. Looking back, I understand that he was trying to push the importance of appreciating life and how there are endless things to do so we should never be bored (or unappreciative). Today, I find me giving myself permission to be bored. The

idea of not having a set to-do list and being able to wander is ideal to me—it sounds kind of perfect.

If we had some time to be bored in our lives, what would we do? What would we discover?

A researcher from the University of Louisville wrote that boredom helps to restore the perception of meaningful activities. He continues to say that "In the absence of boredom, one would remain trapped in unfulfilling situations. . . . Boredom [gives us] a 'push' that motivates us to switch goals and projects."[1] Therefore, being bored and embracing boredom can push us to find the right track for our lives. But to be bored, we must give ourselves a break. I used to fear "being bored," but now I live to find it.

## 11. Always Self-Evaluate

When I prioritize and make decisions about how I will spend my time during the day, I'll ask myself, "At the end of today—what *must* be done? What are my nonnegotiables? What will I be upset about come day's end should I not accomplish it?" These are the activities that I always start with. The feeling of being accomplished at the end of the day and hitting your own goals is *amazing*. Remember to always be evaluating how things are going and your progress (good and bad). Some questions to ask yourself at the end of a long day include:

- What worked?
- What didn't?
- What made you happy?
- What challenged you?
- What's your number one goal for tomorrow?

## 12. Preparation Is Key

A constant theme for me this year has been the word *preparation*. One of my closest friends, Samantha, is a hair stylist
and makeup artist. Last year, she was doing a high-pressure
photo shoot. The models and agents were very particular
about their hair and indecisive about the type of look they
were going for. If I were Samantha, I would have been super
nervous about the entire thing. I remember asking her the
night before the big shoot, "Are you nervous?" She looked at
me and said, "No. I'm prepared."

It turns out Sam had multiple conversations with both
the models and the agents, triple-checked her product sup-
ply, and put enough time in the "getting ready" schedule so
that if anything was wrong, she'd be able to fix it easily. Her
response impressed me so much and made me realize she's
right! If you are prepared, you will be ready and confident for
(almost) anything life will throw your way.

## 13. Celebrate the Good Stuff

When something exciting happens, celebrate it. Life is
short—celebrate the good stuff because we all know that
it's not all good stuff. Part of being your best self is letting
yourself (and others) acknowledge you when something great
happens. When you get too wrapped up in getting it together,
you can get into a focused work zone where you don't want to
do anything except be productive. Take a break and go celebrate yourself—you deserve it!

## 14. Stop Getting Ready to Get Ready

At a certain point, you can only *talk* about doing something for so long. Eventually, you must take action. Stop getting ready to get ready and just go! Here's an example: Let's say I want to write a book. I spend five weeks planning out my book-writing process, making notes on calendars, schedules, and more. I talk to people about how I'm going to write a book. I tell loved ones I'm going to write this book. The conversations and plans continue, but the actual writing never starts. This is what it means when I say, "Stop getting ready to get ready." At some point, I need to stop preparing and just write the book, or else it will never get done. In this book, I talk a lot about planning and a lot about preparation. But at some point, you have to shut up, put your head down, and just get the work done.

## 15. Choose Methods over Moods

Like anyone else, I can get cranky and frustrated. As I wrote this book, I realized the importance of needing to ignore my own moods at times. Before the book, I was quick to make decisions based on my mood. For example, I would think, "I'm tired, so therefore I will decide not to go to the gym." Or "I'm hungry, so I'll eat whatever is in front of me instead of planning a healthy meal." Without fail, every time I chose my mood over my method, I would fall short of completing my goals and end up upset with myself. Today, I've realized this doesn't have to be (and shouldn't be) my default. Instead, I try to make decisions based on my methods, not my moods. My method is my strategy, and it's the way I've determined I can accomplish a goal.

## 16. Use Your Time Wisely

Time is the most valuable thing we have. It's the most precious thing you control. In the book, you'll hear me talk frequently about the importance of time. I believe in taking control of the way we spend our time and taking it very seriously. When we aren't careful, our schedules control us, but with the right amount of thought, preparation, and planning, we can control our schedules. In addition to using your time wisely, be intentional about your time and the way you spend it. Being intentional was a constant theme and came up in almost every interview I conducted for this book. Everyone pushed the importance of setting your intentions for the day first thing and, again, being intentional with how we spend our time.

## 17. Stop Blaming Others

It's easy to blame others for the problems we've brought on ourselves. We must stand up and take responsibility. If I tell someone I will do something in a certain amount of time, and then don't do it, whose fault is that? Mine and mine alone. When you catch yourself playing the blame game (as we all do), take a deep breath and say to yourself, "This is my situation, and I'm going to do what I can to fix it."

• • •

# IT WON'T BE EASY,
# BUT IT WILL BE WORTH IT

Just like anything else, the advice in this book requires patience, trial and error, and for you to push yourself. The way that I got through the work that went into being in a place where I could write this book was by constantly reminding myself of how badly I wanted to feel more together—day in and day out. When you are facing a challenge and don't know the answer, I encourage you to read over these 17 principles. They will serve as a guide and a resource to provide you with the solution you are looking for.

Throughout this book, I'm going to do my part and give you action step upon action step that you can easily implement to change your lifestyle and get it together. But, you and only you must put in the work and think about who you are and who you want to be. I will provide the blueprint for how to get there, but you have to commit to doing the work.

When people say, "You need to get it together!," they don't just mean that you have to be more organized. It's much more than that. It means figuring out who you are and what you want. It means you need to align your actions with your priorities. And that's important. So, I ask you: Who are you? What do you want?

• • •

Writing this book and pushing myself to always follow my own advice hasn't been an easy path, and I don't want to sugarcoat that. If it were easy, everyone would already feel put together.

While family and friends watched me struggle to write this book and practice what I was preaching, they thought I was a little nuts (I think). Out of love, they'd say things like, "Give yourself a break" or "It's not a big deal." But, here's the thing, I've been alive for almost 34 years, and for most of my more "adult" years, I've needed to get it together. I'm not saying that I haven't done anything credible; I know I have. However, there were little things (at work, at home, with my friends, with my family) that I could have been doing better. Now you could argue (as many do) that we all have things that we could do better. Yes, *but* if you could fix half of those things today, wouldn't you try?

I wanted to find ways to remove stress, be happier, feel less overwhelmed, worry less, and feel more put together in general.

I wanted change.

I also wasn't living under a rock. I understand that life isn't always pretty and that sad, tragic, ugly things happen every single day that we can't control. I know that when it rains, it pours, and there's only so much that we can control. Life happens, regardless of whether you're prepared for it. *But*, even with this being true, that doesn't mean we can't clean up what we *can* control in hopes that it will help us feel more together.

To write this book, in the best way I knew how, I opened my heart, swallowed my pride, and decided to put it all out there. I didn't just write this book, I lived this book. I've implemented every plan, tried every tip, and experimented with every piece of advice—and I promise, this stuff can be powerful. These are little steps that can really help you go a long way. More important, these practical tips helped me get from where I was to where I wanted to be: getting it together, one day at time.

I can't wait to help you do the same.

# Chapter 2

## OWN YOUR DAY,
## CLEAN UP
## YOUR ROUTINE

As a little girl, I used to always love playing in my parents' eighties-style bathroom. It was a gigantic room with a huge bathtub, ginormous shower, his and her sinks, and since it was the eighties, completely covered in baby pink bite-sized tiles. Every night, I'd beg to take a bath in their bathtub where I'd pretend to be a television host and narrate my entire nightly routine. First, I'd go into the bathtub and relax for a few minutes. Next, I'd start my hair routine of shampoo and cream rinse (which we now call conditioner). I'd use buckets of the Bath and Body Works Sun-Ripened Raspberry shower gel and scrub myself clean with my hot pink loofa next. Then I'd move to my mother's vanity, where I'd play with her makeup products and explain why and how I was using each one to my fake viewers. I can only imagine how I was using the eye liner and mascara!

Fast-forward 20-something years, and here I am, still obsessed with routines and people's schedules and, of course, eager to share my current daily routine with all of you.

For me, a big part of getting it together has been refining my daily routine. Our routines should reflect the lifestyles that we want to live, not the ones that we've lived to this point. Remember, every single morning we can rewrite our stories and update our daily routines. Let's start today.

Before we dig in, I want to say (again) that I know we're probably not experiencing the exact same life and work styles, but we do have at least one thing in common: we are trying to be the best versions of ourselves that we can possibly be. I'll bet you want to wake up productive and go to bed happy. You want to feel confident instead of anxious. You may even want to make more time for yourself so you can do more of the things you love.

No matter where you are in your career or life, we're all trying to be our authentic selves (whatever that means to you), and while we may not admit it, we're all just trying to figure it out—day by day.

In my interview with Josh Notes, I asked him about his daily routine, and he explained that really nailing down his daily routine was key in finding overall success. He said, "If you win the day, you can win the week. If you can win the week, you can win the month. And, before you know it, you will be winning at life." This statement really got me thinking about my routine and how I use it to win my day, because if you can do that, you will be off to a great start for your life.

• • •

Now, for me to explain how far I've come in creating a schedule that makes me productive, happy, and healthy, I'll have to contrast my new schedule with my former schedule. Before I dive into the "new and improved Lauren," I'll give you a glimpse of what my schedule used to look like when I didn't feel in control of my life or my routine. So, let's rewind the clock a few years and brace yourself for Lauren—the messy days!

## LAUREN: THE MESSY DAYS

My first job after college was super strict and monitored (think asking for permission to go to the bathroom), so when I started my own company, I had no idea how to spend my time. I was used to someone caring about where I was and what I did at all times, so the fact that no one was watching my every move was both liberating and terrifying.

When I met my husband (who is also an entrepreneur), I was in my mid-twenties and had zero employees, so I was my only issue. When we started dating, I remember getting fed up with him when he didn't want to stay out late and would say to him, "What do you mean you have to get up early and go to work tomorrow? You run your own business—you can do anything you want." He was confused. "What do you mean? Of course, I need to go to work. If I want to continue to run my business, I need to do the job—and do it well—every single day," he would say, baffled by my complaint.

"But . . . you make the rules! You can work when you want. Why would you choose to conform?" I would ask because I genuinely didn't understand the need to have a routine to run a productive and effective business.

Needless to say, I learned a ton from him and how he handled his workday. The first thing I learned was that one of my biggest challenges was waking up early. Without having to be somewhere at a specific time or meet someone at a specific place, I found it incredibly challenging to wake up at a decent hour. In addition to that, I worked at my desk that happened to be right next to my bed. During these times, getting up before 10 a.m. seemed impossible.

I also had difficulty managing my priorities and commitments. I didn't keep a calendar. I had the classic "I can remember everything!" mentality, which resulted in me making plans and totally forgetting about half of them. I also thought I could do anything from anywhere, so I'd plan important business calls for times when I knew I'd be on the road or traveling. The outcome? I remember being on the phone with someone from Coach (the handbag company) and driving through the middle of nowhere California on my way to a speaking event. The executive got so frustrated with my poor phone service that he finally just said, "This is unprofessional. We can't do business together."

At the time, I didn't realize how my lack of organization and routine was hurting my professional relationships.

On top of this, I didn't have an office when I started my business, so my getting ready routine didn't exist. I remember worrying to myself, "If I have kids one day, will I ever get dressed? Will I always be the lady in the sweats?" I got so used to putting on a pair of oversized Abercrombie sweatpants, throwing on a big T-shirt from a family vacation that read *Sedona*, bundling up in my dad-like gray hoodie (yes, the same one from the gym), and clipping my hair on top of my head that a friend finally said, "Lauren! You look terrible. Go brush your hair, wash your face, and get it together. You look like a house rat!" And, she was right. (Got to love good friends!) It wasn't until a few years later that I finally started getting dressed regardless of whether I had to leave the house that day.

In addition to being clueless about how to conduct my workday, I was similarly bad at managing a team. Once I started hiring employees, we'd have meetings that would run for hours on end. I remember one of my first employees getting upset because her day was spent having long-winded conversations instead of accomplishing tasks. There was no organization, no systems, and no best practices established. I was basically making everything up as I went.

The changes to my daily routine and breaking my bad habits didn't happen overnight. I'd love to say that I drank some sort of magic potion that suddenly transformed me into the ideal professional, but that wasn't the case. The truth is I worked like that for years. When I think back and ask myself, "What changed?" I don't have a quick answer. I was spending so much time with my now-husband, I slowly began copying his routine. He and his business partner would wake up early, start blasting Stan Getz's "The Girl from Ipanema," get dressed, and start their day hosting conference calls with their teams. And from there, it was off to the races. They'd take a quick break for lunch and then get right back to it.

I'd never really seen entrepreneurs at work in such an up-close way before, so I was fascinated by how they ran their business. Their dedication, motivation, and organization inspired me. I started to wake up when they did, work when they did, take lunch when they did, and finish the workday when they did.

As I started to add structure to my days, I felt my productivity increase. I was landing more calls and more opportunities, and producing content more consistently. And, thanks to their example (shout out to Max Durovic and Mike Kenny of Aarrow Advertising, yes, the now world-famous sign spinners), my work style completely transformed.

• • •

Today, I'm ironically and frequently asked about my routine, my hustle, and generally how I get things done. I'm asked questions including, "How do you balance your family and work so well?" or "How do you run your work meetings, and what kinds of meetings are you in all day?" The other day my husband's grandmother said, "Lauren, how do you have time to pick out your clothes? You always look so put together, but you are always traveling and never home to shop." These questions secretly thrill me because people don't know how long it took me to get it together—and I'm really proud of where I am today.

# A LOOK INTO MY DAY NOW

Now it's time to take you through my new daily routine. I've been following this for about a year and constantly changing, evaluating, and updating it.

Welcome to a day in the life of the new Lauren.

My day technically starts the evening before. Every night, I pick out my clothes for the next day. Sometimes, I pick out my outfits for the entire week over the weekend, so all I have do is lay them out each night. Next, I make sure my gym bag is packed and ready to go (this is also prepped and ready to go before the start of each week). Finally, I get myself mentally prepared for the next day by setting my to-do list ( which I challenge myself to keep to less than five items) and referencing my tools (this includes my Outlook Calendar, inbox, notebook, and project management system— all of which we will talk about in depth in Chapter 5).

## Bonus Tip

Embracing the night before to-do list has been a game changer for me because it serves to illustrate your commitment to tomorrow's self. When I make my to-do list in the morning, I find that it takes me too much time to put together and I already feel behind. Instead, when I write tomorrow's to-do list at the end of the workday when things slow down. I feel like I'm using the best time of my day to plan ahead for the next day. (Make sure this isn't a never-ending to-do list. Nothing will make you feel more extremely unproductive than a list that can never be finished.) We'll discuss to-do lists more in Chapter 5 when we talk about the tools you need for success.

Now that we know what I do the night before, let's look at the start of my day. Today I was up by 6:15. I plopped onto the couch, plugged in my laptop, turned on *Morning Joe*, made coffee, and started working by 6:30 a.m. I try not to have any calls before 8:30 a.m. when we technically "open for business" so I can own my morning time. Remember, time is one of the guiding principles of this journey. Throughout this book you'll hear this mantra over and over—you need to own your time so that it doesn't own you—and starting your day off by setting your own schedule puts this into practice.

I typically start each morning with, a "me project," which is something I want to do and doesn't require a response from someone else. For example, today, I wanted to finish writing a blog for my website, so I started with that and crossed it off my list 20 minutes later.

*Bonus Tip*

I find that if I open my e-mails first thing in the morning, I'm immediately sucked into everyone else's goals and priorities! Of course, you should respond to your e-mails, but you should do it on your own time.

Next, I review my calendar to make sure it's accurate and includes *everything* I need to do for that day. Yes, I did look at it the night before, *but* when I look the night before, I'm typically only looking to see what time my day really starts and when my first morning call or meeting takes place. Now, I'm reviewing to make sure that my day makes sense and my time is being spent in the right ways. I personally e-mail anyone that I have a call or meeting with that day to triple-check that we're confirmed. I find that when you reach out to confirm, people are less likely to cancel. And if they do cancel, you'll avoid sitting on a call waiting for someone who isn't going to show up and wasting your time moving calls around to make a new time fit with your schedule. If there's anything specific I want to send someone before our conversation (such as a meeting agenda or case study), I attach that to the e-mail.

If I'm going to a meeting that day, I make sure that I'm completely aware of how far it is and what time I need to leave. I try to allow 15 to 30 minutes of cushion to avoid stress (and I'm famous for getting lost). I add this travel time to the calendar and make note of things like "LB needs to leave" (LB being me—Lauren Berger). I also try to remove any unnecessary gaps in the day. Most of my tasks can't be done in 20 minutes, so I like to have either large gaps of time that do allow me to do something or no gaps of time.

On an ideal morning, I also take 10 minutes or so to make sure I'm ready for my calls for the day. This makes me feel confident that I'm prepared, whether it be for a business I'm pitching, people I'm speaking with, or any prep work I need to do. I'll also take this time to connect with the people or person I'm meeting on LinkedIn. I find this reminds them that I'm a real person and keeps us connected far past the call itself too. I then check out their company Instagram page and their company website to see what they are featuring and promoting. If I'm responsible for creating an agenda, I also confirm that this is handled and saved inside of the calendar invite (and e-mailed to whoever needs access).

Next, I take out the to-do list that I created the night before and immediately compare it to my calendar. I then look at my day with this in mind: "When am I going to do all of the things on my to-do list?"

A problem I frequently encounter is that I have a to-do list that is completely different from the activities on my calendar. If I'm booked on 30-minute calls all day long, I'll never accomplish the items on my to-do list. So, I go into my calendar and block out time for items on my to-do list. Here's an example. Let's say I must put together a proposal for a client (a task that could take about 25 minutes). This may be a top priority on my to-do list, but if I'm booked all day long, when would I possibly have the time to sit down and do this? Also, proposals aren't exactly easy to create, so I also need to make sure I have the time and space to really focus.

My first step is to look at my calendar to see where I can fit this particular project into my day. If I have the time, I schedule it in right away. If don't, I evaluate other items already on my calendar. I ask myself, "Can any of these be pushed to another time since this proposal is time sensitive?" If the answer is yes, I'll reschedule accordingly. If the answer is no, then I'll need to look at my personal time. How can I fit this into my day without taking away from my other personal activities (exercising, eating dinner, relaxing)? Usually, I can find at least 25 minutes to move around within my day. If I absolutely cannot fit it in, I'll set it as a "Me" task for the following morning. I'll manage the clients' expectations and let them know that I'll be able to send them a proposal by early tomorrow afternoon, as I always want to have some wiggle room.

Sure, things will change and shift each day, but going into work with a serious plan is crucial. If you don't make the most of your day, who will?

Once my day is locked, I scroll through my e-mails from that morning and the evening before to make sure I didn't miss anything pressing. I address urgent e-mails and leave any other e-mails in my inbox for the time being. Remember, I'm working with the mentality that I should be focusing on my priorities, not other people's. Lauryn Hock, influencer and founder of lauryncakes.com, says that she flags her most important e-mails in the morning so they sit on the top of her inbox. This allows her to clearly see her priorities for the day.

Usually by 7:45 a.m., I've wrapped up any urgent situations and I'm ready to execute the daily plan I've created for myself. I'm also minutes away from running late, so I need to get the heck out the door!

First, I put together my workbag, as I don't want that to hold me up as I'm trying to get out of the house. Most of it is already organized, but since I've been working on my computer and with my notebook throughout the morning, I have to wrap up my chargers and put everything back in the bag. (I try to clean the bag out once a week so I avoid the overflowing disaster that it can easily become.)

Then, I head upstairs to get dressed for the day. My goal is to get ready in 15 minutes, 20 if I have a speaking engagement or appearance that day. Because I shower and do my hair the evening before, I don't have to deal with the blow-dryer in the morning. I try to get ready in three to four 5-minute blocks of time, and I must have music playing while I get ready. This sounds crazy, but the music really keeps me on pace while I get ready. If I don't have the music to keep me on track, I end up daydreaming as I put on mascara and completely losing track of the time.

After I'm ready, I grab a banana, yogurt, or oatmeal, or my husband makes egg whites with lots of Sriracha (he's cute!). By this time, I usually mobile order a venti iced coffee to get me through my day. While I order, I eat my breakfast and chat with my husband about our schedules for that day. We like to try to get home around the same time as often as possible.

Next, I'm to the sunglasses bowl where we keep change, sunglasses, and keys. I stole this idea from my sister-in-law after spotting it in her house. It's funny how when you are trying to be more organized with your life, things like sunglasses bowls make you excited! This is a great idea as these items never had a home before.

I'm in the car by exactly 8:23 a.m. (on a good day) with my workbag, gym bag, thermos filled with water, and my iced coffee (which I pick up from a store steps away from where I live). Because I'm always coming in and out of my car with so much stuff in my hands, I try to keep my car as clean as possible. I try to get a car wash once per month and have the "take everything inside at the end of the night" philosophy so I'm not having to perform the dreaded task of cleaning out my car each day.

Lucky for me, my commute is only three to five minutes. Call it a perk of running your own business! I'm big on talking to people while I'm driving (using Bluetooth, of course!), so I call my best friend, Meghan, who lives in Oklahoma. We talk so frequently that we can usually catch up and say hello pretty quickly. (You'll get tons of tips for staying in touch with friends in Chapter 8.)

A few minutes before 8:30, I get to the office. Even though I'm the boss, I try to be on time, not only because I want to set a good example, but in all honesty, I'm truly excited to work with my team! On Mondays, we do our team meetings.

After that, I go right into weekly meetings with the sales and marketing teams to review goals for the coming week. The rest of the day is usually a mix of calls and meetings—these might be pitch calls, sales calls, client calls, internal meetings, press pitches, interviews, collaboration brainstorming calls, and so many other possibilities.

## Bonus Tip

I challenge myself to keep all work calls to 15 minutes (sometimes possible, and sometimes not). I try to establish the goal of the call, reiterate the agenda, ask questions, and understand the next steps. I try to keep my "elevator pitch" under two minutes so that I don't hold up the pace of the call. One of my most popular YouTube videos is called "How to Create Your 30- Second Elevator Pitch"—check it out on our YouTube page (@ internqueen).

Also, if the action items (after a call) are simple, I try to do them right away. For example, if I need to send someone a deck. I can do that immediately following a call, and it takes me less than two minutes. If the action items are more complicated (perhaps I have to write up a proposal or something of that nature), I block out time to work on it within the next one or two business days (and put it on my calendar so that it happens).

Here's a breakdown of my day when I wrote this chapter:

- 8:30 a.m. —Team meeting
- 9:15 a.m. —Sales team meeting
- 9:30 a.m. —Marketing team meeting
- 11:00 a.m. —Sales pitch
- 12:00 p.m. —Informational interview
- 12:30 p.m. —Lunch
- 1:00 p.m. —Do outgoing e-mails/calls/items from my to-do list
- 2:00 p.m. —Pitch call
- 2:30 p.m. —Phone interview with FastCompany.com
- 3:30 p.m. —Internal status meeting
- 4:00 p.m. —Go live on Instagram/Facebook with students from Georgia State College
- 4:15 p.m. —Sign off on YouTube videos from the week
- 4:30 p.m. —Podcast review (from the car, I'm headed home!)
- 5:00 p.m. —Team member call (feelings talk—I try to limit these to only a few minutes to keep it professional)

Because our offices are located on the West Coast in Los Angeles, most of my calls are done in the mornings when the East Coast is still going. Usually by lunchtime (1 p.m. PST/ 4 p.m. EST), things are winding down for our East Coast clients. This makes lunchtime and the second part of my day great for getting through projects and getting some sales e-mails out.

During lunch, my team typically leaves the office and I stay behind. I like the quiet. I turn on music, set a timer, and get out as many sales e-mails as possible to be productive during this time. If there are any personal tasks that I need to get done, I save those for after work (4:30 p.m.) so that I can maximize my time when I'm in the office. Remember, a goal of mine is to get more work done during working hours so that I have less to take home.

After lunch, the team comes back, and I try to meet with them (casually) before the end of the day to review the status on different projects. Even though my company has been around for nine years, we are still a young business and an even younger team. With mostly new team members, I walk a thin line between micromanaging and letting them roam free. Let's just say that I'm still *very* involved.

These meetings used to start at 4 p.m., but we found that we would discover to dos that late in the day, and we ended up

*Bonus Tip*

Because we often have so much to cover in our status meetings at Intern Queen, we have the following rules:

1. One person runs the meeting.
2. No one else can talk during the manager's status updates. Any notes or questions must be written down.
3. Everyone has a timed two to five minutes to go through any questions, problems, or ideas.

The process of having team members (and myself) stop talking and interrupting status updates has taken at least 15 minutes off our meeting times—if not more! These meetings used to turn into what I call "the idea circus" where everyone has an idea about every single item. Now, our meetings are much more productive.

staying at the office several hours later than necessary. Now, we start status checks at around 3 p.m. so that if we run into any issues, we still have time to fix them. Our project management system has really helped streamline tasks and manage our deadlines (more on this in Chapter 5).

• • •

After my workday is over, I like to get the second part of my day moving as quickly as I can. I drive right to the gym, and I call my parents to tell them about the day. (I'll go through my specific gym routine in Chapter 9, but I usually meet a trainer, go to a workout class, or just do some cardio and weight lifting on my own.)

In the car ride home after the gym, I try to drink as much water as possible and make as many of my friend and family phone calls as possible.

Once I'm home (about 7 p.m.), my favorite thing to do is take a walk with my husband around our neighborhood. I love to get his opinions and advice on my day, and I'm eager to hear about his, too. The best part about our walk is that I leave my phone at home! It's our time to be with each other and no one else. As we finish our walk, we'll talk about our plan for that night as it's almost 8 p.m.: What's for dinner? Do we need to work

> ## Bonus Tip
>
> If I'm working during free time, it should be project- or task-based and have a clear start and a clear end. For example, if I'm going to work on my inbox after hours, I wouldn't just say "work on e-mail." Instead, I'd say "answer e-mails from today and yesterday" as that's a finite amount.

more? (The answer is usually yes.) Do we have free time? What shows are we excited to watch that night?

We make dinner together and usually watch TV while eating. This is our "relax and turn off our brains" time. Even though I try to talk to my friends earlier in the day, I always end up chatting with one or two of my closest friends from Los Angeles who work a little later than I do. We all respect one another's work time and try not to create too much of a distraction for each other during the workday.

Finally, by 9 or 10 p.m., I'm back to where we started this section—planning for the next workday, so I can go to bed feeling prepared and having an idea of what's going on the next day at work

## Clean Your Space

While cleaning up your routine is important, working in a clean space is important too. I interviewed Jen Robin, founder of Life in Jeneral, Inc., for her advice on how to get it together and organize yourself at home and at work.

Here are some of her top tips to get organized and clean up your space:

1. Pull everything out and make categories to group like items together. The goal is to have one home for each category (to make everything easy to find and put back).
2. Start with a space or section that will have the most impact on your daily life. Because you use this place every day, it will act as motivation to tackle other spaces.

*(Continued on next page)*

3. As you go through each space, have bins labeled "trash," "donate," and "toss." Get rid of things that are no longer serving you.

4. Once you have settled on what you are keeping, gather items in categories and create *one* home for items in a space that makes the most sense.

5. Whether you go out and buy bins or reuse from around the house, keep categories contained to maintain spaces. Containment is key.

6. If you think you need to purchase anything new for your home, wait. Don't buy anything new until you see what you are missing and really understand what you need.

7. Each day choose one drawer, activity, or even one item to tackle. For example, if there are pencils throughout your workspace, spend 15 minutes gathering all of them and find *one* location to store them all.

8. Change your mindset from finding "quick fixes" to one that embodies living an organized lifestyle.

---

# EVALUATE YOUR ROUTINE

When I follow the daily routine I laid out in this chapter, I go to bed feeling satisfied because I know I got so much accomplished and did my personal best. Once I started taking my daily routine seriously, I was able to design my perfect day slowly and carefully over time.

Now, I'd like you to take some time to think about your own daily routine. Answer the following questions and start your own process of discovering your ideal personal routine:

What's the best part of your "getting ready" routine in the morning that leaves you feeling super productive?

What part of your "getting ready" routine do you want to fix before you finish reading this book? What frustrates you every single morning?

Once you get to work, what is one productive strategy you use to get things done in a timely manner?

Where are you struggling during your daily routine at work? What needs to be improved ASAP?

What specific time in your workday do you feel the most productive? How can you replicate that for other parts of your day?

What time in your day do you feel the least productive? Why do you think that is?

After work, what's your favorite way to spend time?

How is this different from the way you actually spend your time after work?

• • •

Imagine a day when everything goes right from the minute you wake up to the minute you go to bed. Insert your ideal schedule below:

12:00 a.m. _____

1:00 a.m. _____

2:00 a.m. _____

3:00 a.m. _____

4:00 a.m. _____

5:00 a.m. _____

6:00 a.m. _____

7:00 a.m. _____

8:00 a.m. _____

9:00 a.m. _____

10:00 a.m. _____

11:00 a.m. _____

12:00 p.m. _____

1:00 p.m. _____

2:00 p.m. _____

3:00 p.m. _____

4:00 p.m. _____

5:00 p.m. _____

6:00 p.m. _____

7:00 p.m. _____

8:00 p.m. _____

9:00 p.m. _____

10:00 p.m. _____

11:00 p.m. _____

• • •

The following were commonalities that I found when I asked friends about their answers. I think the responses will benefit you.

- "My day isn't normal" or "my life isn't like everyone else's" were the first phrases that I heard from everyone. Everyone thinks her job is special and like none other (sorry, but it's true!). I guess the answer is, your job may be different, but you're experiencing what everyone else is experiencing. While it is true that every job and its requirements are unique, everyone is dealing with stress. Be conscious of this when you work with others. Don't have a pity party for yourself or get stuck in a rut. Help yourself to make the most of your time and get your work done.
- Everyone wants to start the day handling their own priorities and the most effective way to make that happen is to *not* start the day with e-mail. Start your day the way *you* intended, not responding to other people.
- We all want to slow down and wake up earlier. No one likes waking up rushed and worried that they are running late. I hate that feeling! Wake up earlier and get it together.
- People either thrive in the morning when they still feel in control of their day or late in the afternoon, once things get quiet and e-mails slow down. Figuring out where you excel will help you manage your days.

- Everyone's trying to find a balance between running their personal lives and their work lives. It's a struggle, but one that gets better the more you experiment.
- We all want to disconnect. Everyone that I spoke to mentioned wanting to unplug or spend more time on themselves, whether that be with friends, exercising, or just relaxing.

All of these are issues that we will touch on throughout this book. No matter what your concerns are with your schedule, I'm confident that we'll talk through them by the end of this book.

• • •

Every day, is a new opportunity to live your best life.

Your schedule and daily routine is an opportunity to get it together. Just because you had a bad day today doesn't mean you can't change things tomorrow. Reconfiguring your routine is crucial to owning your success and spending your time the way you want. If you take the time to think about your daily routine, you'll discover the ways you should be spending your time to further yourself and get closer to achieving your goals.

As you experiment with your routine, your work, your relationships, and more, you will inevitably experience failure. The next chapter is close to my heart because I share the strategies I use to deal with failure, rejection, and things not going my way. Life can be hard, but have no fear—the next chapter will give you actionable steps and strategies to overcome failure and even start to embrace it. Let's continue!

# *Chapter* 3

# COPING WITH FAILURE

One night, I got out of the shower and just lay on the floor near my bed with my eyes fixated on different parts of my popcorn ceiling. I just lay there. I couldn't move.

Have you ever been there? So stuck in your own shit that you don't have the energy to get off the floor? I have, and it sucks. And usually it's one stupid thing that happened or was said and you just cannot let it go. Questions flood your mind. Why didn't I do the damn laundry? Why couldn't I have just finished my project? Why do I hate everyone at this moment? Why did I get rice in my poke bowl? Why is the scale higher than it should be? Why didn't I do what I said I was going to do?

That day, I stayed on the floor for about 30 minutes frozen in my own anger box. These moments are hard, but I'm here with good news: you can snap out of this.

And, the first step in making that happen is to start *doing* something.

As I've mentioned throughout the book, when I started writing, I didn't feel like I had it together. And trust me, the irony wasn't lost on me. I knew I wanted more control over my own success. I needed my actions to align with my goals.

I need to solidify (once and for all) what my goals and priorities were so that I could successfully plan to achieve them.

I wanted to work on self-love, creating healthy boundaries, coping with failure (obviously), advocating for myself, completing tasks, being more prepared, and acting based on method and not mood. In addition, I wanted to improve the way I worked, focus on personal wellness, increase the amount of time I spent disconnected, and find more time to embrace relaxation (and a little bit of boredom)—quite the list. I could plan and talk about my goals and what I wanted all day, but at some point, I just had to jump in the water and implement my strategies. I was spending too much time getting ready to get ready.

Have you ever jumped in and tried to swim forward, only to find that waves keep coming your way and pushing you back toward the beach? Well, that's me trying to get it together. And on some days, I still feel like that swimmer.

As I went through the trial and error that comes with trying to get it together, I realized that to make significant and lasting change, failure is a requirement. This was not easy for me to accept, but it was necessary to actually make progress.

Things are much better today than they were that day I felt frozen on my floor. All that failure and frustration led me to a place where I now feel in control, aware of how I'm spending my time, more in tune with my own goals, and easily able to recognize how to best use my time. I've aligned my routine and the way I manage my time with the goals I want to achieve, and I'm a better worker, boss, friend, wife, and family member because of it.

A Forbes.com article, "How to Embrace Failure in Order to Become Successful," explains that we can't control what happens, but we can control our reaction to it.[1] And that's really what this chapter is about—it's about how you can control your actions and mindset when you experience failure and some suggested strategies on how to do just that.

## DESCRIBE WHAT YOU EXPERIENCE

First, let's identify some of the negative responses you have when you're in a situation that makes you feel like you're a failure. These are some of my own unhelpful reactions. Please circle any that you can relate to!

- Freaking out
- Having meltdowns
- Getting angry
- Feeling sad
- Ignoring people
- Avoiding fun
- Feeling guilty
- Focusing on the negatives
- Arguing with loved ones
- Sleeping

It's helpful to document these reactions so you can identify them in the future. What are some of your bad habits when it comes to coping with failure? List them here:

_____

_____

_____

# EMBRACE REJECTION

Whenever I speak, I tell audience members not to fear rejection. I tell them that even when you're "successful" you still get rejected. I'm rejected every single day. Sometimes the rejections aren't a big deal and I brush them off. Other times, they hurt.

Just last week, I faced rejection, and the e-mail with the news really stung. For the past three years, we've worked with a big brand sponsor on our annual Intern Queen Party (our free summer event for interns in New York City and Los Angeles). Last year, we put together two events that were top-notch. They were filled with hundreds of ambitious college students, high-level executives, inspirational content, special social media moments, and major engagement. I was proud of the hard work my team and I put in—and confident we impressed the sponsor. Last month, I got an e-mail from the sponsor. This same executive that once greenlit the party (and made me so happy) only three years back was now the same person rejecting a future partnership.

"Unfortunately, we'll be unable to support the Intern Queen Party Series moving forward," he wrote in this e-mail. Ouch. A painful feeling ran through my body. I put my heart and soul into events, and to work so hard only to hear that your sponsor is pulling out really stinks. But there was a silver lining: I was confident because I knew we did everything we could to make those events successful. Once I got over the initial rejection, I responded to the sponsor's e-mail. Here's how I handled it:

- **Avoid immediate responses.** When you are upset, give yourself a minute to assess the situation and come up with a productive response. If you respond immediately, you might say something you'll regret.
- **Read it a few times.** Sometimes when we get bad news, we only read certain parts of the e-mail. Read the entire e-mail a few times to make sure you aren't missing any key words.
- **Pause.** Another way to avoid immediate responses is to pause. Take a deep breathe, go outside, work out, or switch gears. Whatever you decide, just do something else for a bit.
- **Vent correctly.** When you vent, do it with the right person. Don't vent to someone who is above you in ranking or who might not understand your feelings. This could make you more upset. Welcome any advice, but think on it and again, avoid immediate responses.
- **Separate yourself from your job.** Remind yourself, this isn't personal, it's business. This isn't a personal dig or an attack on you personally.

- **When you're ready, reply.** After taking a few days off from considering this e-mail, sit down with a fresh, positive perspective and respond. Always be kind and respectful. Remember, you never want to burn a bridge.
- **Turn the problem into an opportunity.** In Ryan Holiday's article "Why You Should Embrace Failure" from *Psychology Today*, he discusses how failures can be painful in the short term and are beneficial in the long term. "Problems become opportunities," he says.[2] And he's right. Just because this sponsor didn't want to work with me doesn't mean I can't find others. And that's the opportunity—to go find more sponsors and not let this rejection get me down.

Going back to my sponsor e-mail: I did all the above, and two days later, I was ready to respond with a gracious note. Want to read it?

> Hi Richard,
> I *so* appreciate your e-mail and transparency. We've had a great run with (*sponsor*) and hope you are happy with the success of the program. I'll always be fond of you and I appreciate your faith in me—and my company. Thanks for opening your doors to our students. I know they've appreciated the opportunity. I attached last year's recap just so you have it on file. Should future opportunities arise, please think of us. I'm excited for our paths to cross again!
>
> Best,
> Lauren

In case you were wondering, I never got a response to this e-mail, but I was happy with my response. I was professional, I left the door open for a future relationship, and I was kind and appreciative of his help up to that point in time. In situations like this, remember that you can only control yourself and your own actions. I'm proud of how I handled this difficult situation.

## UNDERSTAND YOUR FRUSTRATIONS

Dealing with rejection is hard. No one enjoys feeling like they've failed. But, focusing on what we're feeling is very important in this process. Below are some of the reasons I get upset with myself:

- Hard work, no results
- The people around me don't get it
- Stupid mistakes
- Feeling irresponsible (like I knew better)
- Jealousy
- When something happens in our lives that we can't control (sickness, death, trauma, accidents)

What about you? What makes you get upset with yourself? Write down the top three reasons why you get frustrated with yourself.

_____

_____

_____

Now, I want you to ask yourself another question: What can I do to overcome these frustrations? How can I better handle these when they happen?

We tend to get frustrated by the same things repeatedly. If we can identify the things that frustrate us, prepare for them, and have active solutions to turn to, we may be able to minimize the amount of frustration we deal with on a daily basis.

## HOW TO COPE WITH FAILURE EFFECTIVELY

In that same *Psychology Today* article, Ryan Holiday says that in Silicon Valley engineers look at failure as a positive. He says, "Failure . . . is the feature that precedes nearly all successes,"[3] meaning that to succeed, you have to fail first. I can personally relate to this piece of advice as everything that I've done that people would call "successful" started with failure.

But how can we take this advice and apply it to the small failures that we oftentimes experience? When's the last time you lost your wallet or driver's license or totally forgot about a meeting, appointment, or family member's birthday? We've all experienced that feeling, that "I'm an asshole" feeling, when we mess up. But how can we shake it?

If we think back to Ryan Holiday's "failure is a feature" piece of advice, we must remind ourselves that this is a lesson and our takeaway should be that we won't make the same mistake again. Now that we've failed, we should learn our lesson and be successful in this part of our life moving forward. Perhaps that means never taking our ID out of our wallet or always zipping our handbag so nothing falls out. Perhaps it means checking our calendar every morning to triple-check that we don't miss anything or starting to put our personal commitments in our calendars as soon as plans are finalized. No matter the solution, find the best way to fix the issue and then follow your own advice. Doing so allows you to turn failure into success.

Every day, we experience things we can control and things that we can't. I deal with failure daily. As someone who puts herself out there constantly (pitching new executives, students, businesses, and schools), I'm constantly told no and always facing rejection. I try to take my own advice and handle these situations in constructive and healthy ways, but I want to be honest with you too, I'm not always perfect— not even close. Some rejections are harder to deal with than others, but applying these techniques will allow us to grow stronger and more resilient together.

My friend and efficiency expert Josh Notes appears uber-confident all of the time. When I interviewed him for this book, I asked how he deals with rejection. (Even though I couldn't imagine Josh being rejected.) Josh said, "When I'm losing my shit and not in control, I pull the car over and meditate." That's his secret! He says he almost always feels better quickly. He also expressed the importance of just "letting go." He says, "You have to let go of your bad shot in order to find a great one." This really stuck with me.

Try the following techniques to effectively let go of a bad situation in order to find the next great one.

## Plan, Measure, Tweak, Repeat

Whenever you try to do something new, there's a risk of failure. It's important to have an Action Plan, follow it, and measure your results. If the results don't reflect your ultimate goal, you have to switch up the plan. For example, if I'm trying to get new business by doing a certain number of cold e-mails each month, and I do this for two months and see no results, it's my job to take note and try something new. Failure happens, but it's your job to tweak the plan once you see a lack of success or results.

## Remind Yourself Other Opinions Don't Matter

When we're experiencing failure or rejection and vent to loved ones, it's frustrating when they don't get it. My advice here is to take it with a grain of salt and to remind yourself that they don't have to get it. When I'm trying to explain something to friends and want their feedback, I'll try to give them an example centered in their own life. By explaining it to them in a way they can understand and relate to, I'll probably get a better response and better results.

## Speak to Someone Who Gets It

I've talked about this a few times throughout the book, but vent to the right people. Those who understand you and your business will relate to what you're experiencing and be your best supporters. When I'm having what I call "work drama," I call my friends who also run small businesses and have small teams. They can relate to my issue and might have experience dealing with it themselves. Typically, I'd call Rachel Doyle, founder and CEO of GlamourGals, whom I reference a few times in the book, or my close friend Alyson Roy, founder of AMP3 Public Relations.

## Stop Jealousy

Jealousy and self-doubt must be cut off at the source—immediately! First, turn off the social media, as this is a source of many jealous feelings. (We'll talk about this more in Chapter 7.) Next, tell yourself to *stop*. We have no time for these feelings. Finally, ask yourself what exactly you are jealous of. How can you focus on you? In the next chapter we'll discuss goal-setting. This exercise will help you spend time focusing on what you are trying to accomplish instead of watching what other people are working on.

## Take Action!

What's the latest and greatest problem you are facing at home or at work? Instead of complaining about it and moping around, how can you take action and fix it?

Let's look at an example of this in action. Your boss is upset because you've been late to work for the past few weeks and she wants you to be more punctual. You have a laundry list of reasons why you've been late (including traffic, lost your keys, your dog wasn't behaving, and you woke up late). What are some steps you can take to proactively fix the problem? (1) You could wake up 15 minutes earlier (not a huge change, but it could help you get out the door faster). (2) You could pack your workbag and pick out your clothes the night before (so that process doesn't hold you up). (3) You could set an alarm on your phone for the time when you need to be starting your commute.

By coming up with an Action Plan, you are proactively solving your problem instead of just complaining about it.

## Focus on You

Do you sometimes feel yourself getting caught up in another person's drama? The best remedy is to focus on yourself. Ask yourself, "How can I improve? How can I help move the needle for the team?" Try not to focus on what's happening around you, as you can't control others. Instead, focus on yourself and your professional growth. In the next chapter, I'll help you build your personal goals. Get excited!

## Don't Stray from Routine

Avoid throwing your hands up in the air and letting something small ruin your entire day. The success of your day isn't based on the number of mistakes you make, so when bumps in the road appear, stay on track and continue your day. I'm guilty of having a big schedule for myself (for a specific workday) and just getting so thrown by something, someone, or some e-mail—and then literally self-destructing and going to sleep for the rest of the day. This is *not* the way to deal with failure. Instead, take a deep breath and let your schedule guide you through the rest of your day. I promise, keeping the ship moving will help.

## Keep It in Perspective

If you are reading this book, you probably struggle between your work life and your personal life. You probably feel like you work all of the time—and like you are just getting it wrong. When you feel like a failure or you face rejection, you have to put it all in perspective. Yes, at the very moment something happens, we all think it's the biggest deal in the world. But at the end of the day, will this matter in one week? One month? One year? Ten years? Usually, the answer is no. Remind yourself that you are not your job and you aren't defined by where you work or how you work. You are you— regardless of the mistake you made, client you lost, or deal that didn't go through. You are bigger than your job. Don't forget that.

## Have a Conversation About Something Totally Different

If I'm feeling too "in it" with work and life, having a super random conversation gets me out of the rut I'm stuck in.

For example, I'll do things like call a friend and talk about how her baby is doing, go on a celebrity website to read some mindless gossip, or call my brother to talk about his wedding plans. No matter what you choose to do, make sure it serves as a reminder to yourself that work isn't your entire life.

## Treat Yourself

What are some small things that you enjoy? When you are feeling down, make sure to treat yourself. This doesn't mean that you must buy yourself something expensive, it means go to your favorite coffee shop, go to your favorite sushi spot for dinner, or sneak in some yummy ice cream that night. Just do something nice for yourself that you will truly enjoy. Give yourself a break!

## Remind Yourself You've Failed Before and Got Through It

When failure happens, it can feel like the end of the world. At times we all need to remind ourselves that we've been here before and it all worked out one way or another. Just like last time, you will handle it and find a way to make it better. At this point in my career, I've learned that oftentimes getting to where you want to be comes from several rounds of failure and rejection. Years ago, when I went to write my first book (*All Work, No Pay*), I got the nastiest e-mails from potential agents and publishers telling me that my work wasn't important and would never be published. Just a few years after that, I connected with a great agent (whom I still work with today), and we found an amazing publisher. In a sense, rejection has helped me get from where I was to where I wanted to be.

The other night I was feeling down about our sales numbers for the year—they aren't exactly where I'd like them to be. It's been one of those weeks when it feels like every single person I pitch is rejecting me. But I had to remind myself, I'd been here before. And not just one time—several other times. Now that I've been in business for so many years, I understand that sometimes there are slumps, but keep putting yourself out there and you'll find that *yes*. Reminding myself of the past and that I'd already been here and conquered this situation really helped me see the brighter side of the situation.

## Remember That Rejection Doesn't Mean Never

Another lesson that I've learned is that you will get rejected from companies, deals, clients, colleagues, and opportunities, but that rejection doesn't necessarily last forever. Meaning that the people who say no to you one time may return in the future to say yes. In my career, I've seen this play out time and time again. I'll get rejected from certain opportunities for years, and because of my strong follow-up game, I'll actually stay in touch with the person and eventually turn the no into a yes.

## A, B, C It

Kill the anxiety by writing out or listing out the options and scenarios. When an unexpected situation arises or life isn't going the way you want, come up with A, B, C plans. Having backup plans in place that are always ready to be activated helps me deal with stressful situations. This actually worked out really well for me recently. I was trying to find a new sponsor for that event series that we discussed earlier, and we are coming up to our internal deadline. I was starting to feel worried that we wouldn't be able to find a sponsor, so I came up with the following A, B, C plan so I didn't overstress about it:

**A.** Follow up with everyone that's shown interest and remind them of the deadline.
**B.** Go out to 50 new potential sponsors ASAP just so that I know I did my best in trying to find a sponsor.
**C.** If I don't hear back by Friday, start making calls and trying to find donated event space and vendors who want to participate for trade. This way, I can still have the events, we just won't have a sponsor.

• • •

Take some time to think about situations in which you faced failure. How did you deal with them effectively? List these methods (or potential methods that you might want to try) on the following lines. This will serve as an invaluable reference the next time you face failure.

_____

_____

_____

# PUTTING EVERYTHING INTO PERSPECTIVE

As you work on getting it together, it's important to remember that while we can try our best to control our schedules, plans, calendars, and how frequently we get to the gym, life happens—and usually at the worst times. We've all been there . . . whether it's getting sick, coping with a death in the family, dealing with an upset client, or being delayed by a hurricane or snowstorm, life happens to everyone. By getting a better grip on the stuff we can control (such as how much sleep we get), we'll be better equipped to deal with anything that comes our way.

If we can handle the small things, we'll be better prepared to deal with the big things.

By understanding how to effectively handle rejection and failure, you'll have the tools you need to continuously experiment and try new things as we work to get it together. Let's dive right in with Chapter 4, "Set Your Goals."

# *Chapter* 4

## SET YOUR GOALS

**B**efore you can really be productive, you have to know what you are trying to accomplish. In this section, we will stop, think, create a plan, and set goals in order to be more productive.

We can't just operate blindly each day—we have to know what needs to be done and what we're working toward. Goal-setting is crucial to your success and your sanity when it comes to getting it together—and that's exactly what we'll be doing in this chapter.

## SMART GOALS

A great way to set effective goals is to make sure they are SMART: specific, measurable, achievable, relevant, and time bound. Robert Rubin, a professor at Saint Louis University, explains that SMART goals are important because they ensure that "your goals are clear and reachable."[1] He goes on to say that each goal should be SMART:

- **Specific (simple, sensible, significant).** *Note:* In my goals that we will discuss later in this chapter, I didn't just say I want to lose weight. (Ha! Yep, that's coming!). I listed exactly how many pounds I wanted to lose.
- **Measurable (meaningful, motivating).** *Note:* These goals should be things that you genuinely want to achieve—and measurable so you compare where you are to where you need to be.
- **Achievable (agreed, attainable).** *Note:* What fun is a goal if it's super easy to accomplish? What fun is a goal if it's not actually possible to achieve? If you look at my goals, you'll notice that I said I wanted to lose 5 pounds in a year. I chose this time frame and number because they are realistic.
- **Relevant (reasonable, realistic and resourced, results-based).** *Note:* Make sure these goals are relevant to you. If you cannot relate to your own goals, you'll experience a disconnect and you won't be passionate about reaching them.
- **Time bound (time-based, time limited, time/cost limited, timely, time-sensitive).** *Note:* In the goal exercise on the following page, I ask you to set goals with time frames in mind because all goals you set for yourself should have some sort of time constraint or deadline.

# SET YOUR GOALS

Now that you know your goals have to be SMART, use the space provided below to jot down 10 potential goals for yourself. Don't worry about the order they are in or anything else; just get all of your ideas out of your head and onto paper. These goals should be a mix of personal and professional aspirations that put you and what you want out of life first and foremost.

1. _____

2. _____

3. _____

4. _____

5. _____

6. _____

7. _____

8. _____

9. _____

10. _____

Now really take a look at your 10 goals and ask yourself these questions:

- Can any of these goals be grouped into one? For example, if you wrote "lose weight" and "go to the gym more," find a way to group them together!

- Are you really excited to accomplish some more than others?
- Do you need to accomplish certain goals sooner than others?

With your answers in mind, narrow these 10 goals down to your *top three* for the next 12 months. I know this can be hard, but having a manageable set of goals that you can remember is crucial in actually achieving them. If you aren't ready to set your goals just yet and are looking for some inspiration, take a look at my own goals in the next section. They may spark some ideas!

When you are ready, use the space below to write down your three goals for the next year. Just make sure they are specific, measureable, attainable, relevant, and time bound!

**1.** _____

**2.** _____

**3.** _____

## Your YQMB

*Congratulations!* You've set your three personal (and SMART) goals for the next year. This is an important first step in getting it together. Now we need to set a process for actually making these goals a reality! I'll show you exactly how to do this through my own goal-setting process: YQMB.

Your YQMB goals—or yearly, quarterly, monthly, and biweekly goals—are going to be the launching point for the rest of this book. These goals will guide your daily activities, time, and attention. Writing them down over and over again is helpful, but I don't want you to just write down your goals. I also want you to shout them from the rooftops and know them like the back of your hand. As I've said, if you don't know your goals, who will?

• • •

The rest of this chapter is dedicated to creating your own personal strategy to reach your goals. Together, we'll break your goals down into tangible steps, create a personalized Action Plan, and design a Time Chart to help evaluate how you're spending your time now versus how you actually want to spend your time.

So, grab a pen and mark up these following pages with your notes. If you prefer not to write in your book, that's fine, too. Just grab some paper and follow along there.

One last thing before we get started, though. You are about to do some really hard work. It might be tempting to skip the work in this chapter and just move to the next, but I highly encourage you not to. The work we will do together in the coming pages will push you to engage, interact, and connect with what's most important to you.

Are you ready to reach your goals? Let's dive in.

### Yearly (Y)

While we already set our yearly goals, but writing each one down multiple times will help you to remember them! As a reference, you will see my yearly goals labeled "Lauren's Y." Fill in your own yearly goals in the space below marked "My Y."

---

**Lauren's Y**

1. Y: Take Intern Queen revenues to $2 million for the year.
2. Y: Lose 5 pounds.
3. Y: Speak in front of 1,000 new students (for Intern Queen).

---

**My Y**

1. Y: _____
2. Y: _____
3. Y: _____

---

### Yearly and Quarterly (YQ)

The next step in this process is breaking down our yearly goals into four parts: our quarterly goals. For this step, simply take each of your yearly goals and divide them into four smaller parts. For example, if I want to get in front of 1,000 students in one year, I would divide that by four and get a quarterly goal of reaching 250 students.

It's important to note that your quarterly goals can and likely will change from quarter to quarter. If your goal is to ride your bike 100 miles over the course of a year, you may not be able to log 25 miles in the winter because of snow! Think about this as you set your quarterly goals.

If one of your goals doesn't have a number attached to it, I encourage you to find a way to attach a number because tracking your progress this way will be much easier (and specific, as we learned in our SMART goals). Let's say your goal is to follow your morning routine consistently. That's a wonderful goal, but hard to measure with no numeric values behind it. You just need to put a number on it. Perhaps a percentage. You could say, "I'm going to follow my morning routine 80 percent of each month." This means you'd follow your routine 24 days out of the month and track your progress on a calendar or planner.

Oh, and one last note: don't worry about finding the "perfect time" to get started (like January first or your birthday), just do it now!

Use my quarterly goals as an example and fill in your own on the following page:

---

**Lauren's YQ**

1. Y: Take Intern Queen revenues to $2 million for the year.
   Q: Reach quarterly revenues of $500,000.
2. Y: Lose 5 pounds.
   Q: Lose 1.25 lbs each quarter.
3. Y: Speak in front of 1,000 new students (for Intern Queen).
   Q: Speak in front of 250 new students each quarter.

**My YQ**

1. Y: _____

   Q: _____

2. Y: _____

   Q: _____

3. Y: _____

   Q: _____

### Weekly, Quarterly, and Monthly (YQM)

The next step in this process is setting monthly goals. Here, you will divide each quarterly goal into three months.

For example, I know that I want to reach 1,000 students in one year and 250 students each quarter. If I break this down even further, my monthly goal would be to reach 83 new students.

At the end of each month, I am to achieve that goal. If I realize I didn't achieve what I hoped, I reassess my goal for next month and make adjustments as needed. Set aside one day a month (maybe the last Sunday of each month) to make sure your monthly goals are still in line so you can achieve those quarterly goals.

Use my monthly goals as an example and fill in your own below:

---

**Lauren's YQM**

1. Y: Take Intern Queen revenues to $2 million for the year.
   Q: Reach quarterly revenues of $500,000.
   M: Reach monthly revenues of $167,000.
2. Y: Lose 5 pounds.
   Q: Lose 1.25 lbs each quarter.
   M: Lose .5 lbs each month.
3. Y: Speak in front of 1,000 new students (for Intern Queen).
   Q: Speak in front of 250 new students each quarter.
   M: Speak in front of 83 new students each month.

---

**My YQM**

1. Y: _____
   Q: _____
   M: _____
2. Y: _____
   Q: _____
   M: _____
3. Y: _____
   Q: _____
   M: _____

*Weekly, Quarterly, Monthly, and Biweekly (YQMB)*

I personally think that a week is too short a time to see major results, so instead I set biweekly goals. For this step in the process, take your monthly goals and divide them in half.

To continue our example, I know that I want to reach 1,000 students in one year, 250 students each quarter, and 83 new students a month. If I take that to our last step, I need to reach 41 new people every two weeks.

As I do with my monthly goals, I regularly check in to make sure I'm on track. I use my Sunday nights to look over my YQMB goals, see how close I am to hitting my biweekly goal, and plan my week accordingly (we'll get to more on this soon). If I need to adjust, tweak, or evaluate any biweekly goals or Action Plans, I do this on Sunday night as well.

---

**Lauren's YQMB**

1. Y: Take Intern Queen revenues to $2 million for the year.
   Q: Reach quarterly revenues of $500,000.
   M: Reach monthly revenues of $167,000.
   B: Reach biweekly revenues of $83,000.
2. Y: Lose 5 pounds.
   Q: Lose 1.25 lbs each quarter.
   M: Lose .5 lbs each month.
   B: Focus on that .5 goal for the month on a biweekly basis (technically lose .25 biweekly)
3. Y: Speak in front of 1,000 new students (for Intern Queen).
   Q: Speak in front of 250 new students each quarter.
   M: Speak in front of 83 new students each month.
   B: Speak in front of 41 new students biweekly.

---

**My YQMB**

1. Y: _____

   Q: _____

   M: _____

   B: _____

2. Y: _____

   Q: _____

   M: _____

   B: _____

3. Y: _____

   Q: _____

   M: _____

   B: _____

---

• • •

Now memorize these goals.

Seriously, pause here and say them aloud. I can't tell you how many times I've asked people about their own goals and they don't know the answer. I want you to be able to recite your goals to yourself and anyone who asks immediately and confidently. You got this, so let's keep going.

## Creating a Plan: Actions and Time

*Phew!* You have done a ton of hard work so far! You should be proud of the time, focus, and energy it took to set these goals for yourself.

Now, I'd like to help you take these goals one step further and determine what *actions* you need to take and how much *time* you need to set aside to achieve your YQMB goals.

### Actions

Using your Y and B goals as starting points, determine three steps you need to take over the next two weeks that will help you achieve your B goals. Take a look at my own Action Plan for each of my goals on the next page. At any time if you feel like your action steps aren't working, revise immediately.

It's important to note that the steps in your Action Plan can stay the same *or* change every two weeks. This will depend on your goal (and if you are on or off track to reach it). The biggest thing to keep in mind here is that your Action Plan should always reflect what you are trying to accomplish over a two-week period. If you do that, you'll be on the right track.

## GOAL #1

Y: Take Intern Queen revenues to $2 million for the year.
B: Reach biweekly revenues of $83,000.

---

**Action Plan**

---

*(The steps I'd like to take over a two-week period)*
1. Send 900 e-mails to brands I'm trying to pitch.
2. Check LinkedIn for new leads and opportunities and find at least 50 e-mail addresses.
3. Follow up with old clients and e-mails and send out 100 follow-ups.

---

## GOAL #2

Y: Lose 5 pounds.
B: Lose half a pound biweekly.

---

**Action Plan**

---

1. Work out at least six times over a two-week period.
2. Eat clean for 32 out of 42 meals.
3. Take two workout classes over a two-week period (perhaps try new ones)!

## GOAL #3

Y: Speak in front of 1,000 new students.

B: Speak in front of 41 new students biweekly.

---

### Action Plan

1. Speak in front of two student organizations every two weeks (one per week).
2. Evaluate each engagement to see which groups enjoy my talks the most.
3. E-mail 20 groups every two weeks to book more presentations.

---

Take the time and determine your own Action Plan in the space provided:

## GOAL #1

Y: _____

B: _____

---

### Action Plan

1. _____

2. _____

3. _____

## GOAL #2

Y: _____

B: _____

---

**Action Plan**

1. _____

2. _____

3. _____

---

## GOAL #3

Y: _____

B: _____

---

**Action Plan**

1. _____

2. _____

3. _____

### *Time*

Now that we know what we have to do thanks to our Action Plan, the next step is to determine how much time these action steps will take over a two-week period.

To get started, look at each individual step in your Action Plan and determine how much time that task will take (over a two-week span). Now, give yourself a little wiggle room and overestimate that time by four hours. Keep in mind that this Action Plan is for a two-week period, so if I think it will take 7 hours to send 900 e-mails, I will overestimate by 4 hours to get 11 hours per two-week period.

Next, I want you to include how many days it will take you to complete this particular goal and overestimate this number by two days. This will ensure that you plan enough time to accomplish each step of your action plan. For the example above, I would write "11 hours/6 days" next to my biweekly goal of sending 900 e-mails (even though I actually think this will take me 7 hours over 4 days).

If you need more than 14 days to complete a step on your action plan, you'll need to reassess your Action Plan. Remember, we want to create goals we can achieve over a two-week period.

Here's a look into my own Action Plan for each of my goals:

## GOAL #2

Y: _____

B: _____

**Action Plan**

1. _____

2. _____

3. _____

## GOAL #3

Y: _____

B: _____

**Action Plan**

1. _____

2. _____

3. _____

## *Time*

Now that we know what we have to do thanks to our Action Plan, the next step is to determine how much time these action steps will take over a two-week period.

To get started, look at each individual step in your Action Plan and determine how much time that task will take (over a two-week span). Now, give yourself a little wiggle room and overestimate that time by four hours. Keep in mind that this Action Plan is for a two-week period, so if I think it will take 7 hours to send 900 e-mails, I will overestimate by 4 hours to get 11 hours per two-week period.

Next, I want you to include how many days it will take you to complete this particular goal and overestimate this number by two days. This will ensure that you plan enough time to accomplish each step of your action plan. For the example above, I would write "11 hours/6 days" next to my biweekly goal of sending 900 e-mails (even though I actually think this will take me 7 hours over 4 days).

If you need more than 14 days to complete a step on your action plan, you'll need to reassess your Action Plan. Remember, we want to create goals we can achieve over a two-week period.

Here's a look into my own Action Plan for each of my goals:

## GOAL #1

Y: Take Intern Queen revenues to $2 million for the year.
Q: Reach quarterly revenues of $500,000.
M: Reach monthly revenues of $167,000.
B: Reach biweekly revenues of $83,000.

| Action Plan | Time |
| --- | --- |
| **1.** Send 900 e-mails. | 11 hours /6 days |
| **2.** Check LinkedIn for new leads and opportunities and find at least 50 e-mail addresses. | 9 hours/7 days |
| **3.** Follow up with old clients and e-mails and send out 100 follow-ups. | 9 hours/7 days |

## GOAL #2

Y: Lose 5 pounds.
Q: Lose 1.25 lbs each quarter.
M: Lose .5 lbs each month.
B: Focus on that .5 goal for the month on a biweekly basis (technically lose .25 biweekly)

| Action Plan | Time |
| --- | --- |
| **1.** Work out at least six times. | 10 hours/8 days |
| **2.** Eat clean for 32 out of 42 meals. | 10 hours/10 days<br>*(Includes grocery shopping, cooking, searching recipes, etc.)* |
| **3.** Take two workout classes. | 4 hours/4 days |

## GOAL #3

Y: Speak in front of 1,000 new students (for Intern Queen).
Q: Speak in front of 250 new students each quarter.
M: Speak in front of 83 new students each month.
B: Speak in front of 41 new students biweekly.

| Action Plan | Time |
|---|---|
| 1. Speak in front of two student organizations every two weeks. | 6 hours/2 days |
| 2. Evaluate each engagement to see which groups enjoy my talks the most. | 4 hours/2 days |
| 3. E-mail 20 groups to secure new presentations. | 6 hours/2 days |

Now, do the same for yourself!

## GOAL #1

Y: _____

Q: _____

M: _____

B: _____

| Action Plan | Time |
|---|---|
| 1. _____ | _____ |
| _____ | _____ |
| _____ | _____ |
| 2. _____ | _____ |
| _____ | _____ |
| _____ | _____ |
| 3. _____ | _____ |
| _____ | _____ |
| _____ | _____ |

## GOAL #2

Y: _____

Q: _____

M: _____

B: _____

| Action Plan | Time |
|---|---|
| 1. _____ | _____ |
| _____ | _____ |
| _____ | _____ |
| 2. _____ | _____ |
| _____ | _____ |
| _____ | _____ |
| 3. _____ | _____ |
| _____ | _____ |
| _____ | _____ |

## GOAL #3

Y: _____

Q: _____

M: _____

B: _____

| Action Plan | Time |
| --- | --- |
| 1. _____ | _____ |
| _____ | _____ |
| _____ | _____ |
| 2. _____ | _____ |
| _____ | _____ |
| _____ | _____ |
| 3. _____ | _____ |
| _____ | _____ |
| _____ | _____ |

## Create a Time Chart

Now that we've set our Action Plan and decided how much time we think each part of our plan will take, we need to determine how to fit all of this into our already busy lives on a biweekly basis!

I know this can be daunting right now, but your Time Chart will be a lifesaver!

While this Time Chart is optional, I strongly encourage you to at least try it! I love seeing this layout of how I spend my time.

| 1 | 2 | 3 | 4 | 5 |
|---|---|---|---|---|
| What are you spending your time on? | # of Hours Week 1 | # of Hours Week 2 | Total | Percentage (total/336) |
| IQ Revenue AP | 20 | 20 | 40 | 12% |
| Fitness | 12 | 12 | 24 | 7% |
| Building Superfans | 10 | 10 | 20 | 6% |
| Work with Teams | 11 | 11 | 22 | 6% |
| Speaking to Students | 8 | 8 | 16 | 5% |
| Creating Content | 8 | 8 | 16 | 5% |
| E-mails | 13 | 13 | 26 | 8% |
| Social Media | 5 | 5 | 10 | 3% |
| Texting | 4 | 4 | 8 | 2% |
| Family/Friends | 13 | 13 | 26 | 8% |
| Relaxation | 12 | 12 | 24 | 7% |
| Sleep | 42 | 42 | 84 | 25% |
| Eating | 10 | 10 | 20 | 6% |
| **TOTAL** | | | | **100%** |

Inspired to create your own? Follow the directions below to make your very own Time Chart.

**Step 1:** Break down how you spend your time right now. For me, this includes e-mails, social media, texting, family and friends, relaxation, sleep, working with team members at Intern Queen, and creating content.

**Step 2:** Add the ways you spend your time in Column 1.

**Step 3**: Continue adding to Column 1 by writing in your yearly goals.

**Step 4:** Estimate how much time you will spend on each project during Week 1. Add this number to Column 2.

**Step 5:** Estimate how much time you will spend on each project during Week 2. Add this number to Column 3.

**Step 6:** Add the hours from Columns 2 and 3 together. Write this number in Column 4.

**Step 7**: Divide the number in Column 4 by 336 (as there are 336 hours in a two-week period). Write this final number in Column 5.

**Step 8:** Add up the numbers in Column 5 and make sure your total is 100 percent! If it's not, adjust your schedule accordingly.

| 1 | 2 | 3 | 4 | 5 |
|---|---|---|---|---|
| What are you spending your time on? | # of Hours Week 1 | # of Hours Week 2 | Total | Percentage (total/____) |
| | | | | |
| | | | | |
| | | | | |
| | | | | |
| | | | | |
| | | | | |
| | | | | |
| | | | | |
| | | | | |
| | | | | |
| | | | | |
| TOTAL | | | | 100% |

**Optional Bonus Step:** While this step is optional, I find that it's really helpful to have a visual understanding of your time. You can create your own Time Pie Graph like mine on the following page by drawing one big circle and dividing it into the percentages you just created in your Time Chart. If you are looking for a more exact pie chart, open Microsoft Excel and type each of the things you are spending your time on in one column and the corresponding percentage in the next. Select all of the boxes you just typed in, select "insert" at the top of the page, and select Pie Charts, and Excel will generate an exact graph for you!

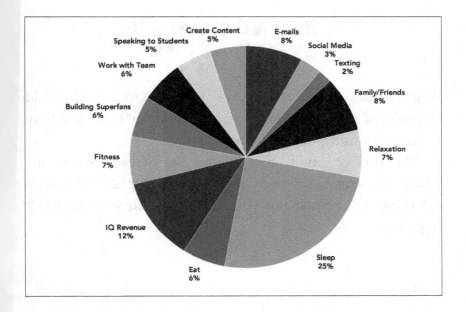

Give this a try in the blank circle below!

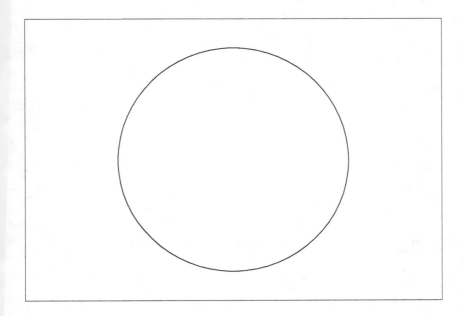

Voilà! You're done!

# TIME AND GOALS IN
# EVERYDAY LIFE

*Wow!* We did a lot of work together in this chapter. You should be proud of yourself! You've created your very own road map to success—and a detailed one at that.

The work you did in this chapter clarified where you currently are, where you want to be, and your plan for how to get there. You've just put yourself on a clear path to get it together.

• • •

In the next chapter I'll be walking you through the tools you can use to make sure you keep up with these goals and get it together. Let's keep going!

# *Chapter* 5

# THE TOOLS

**W**hy can't we get it together at work? Why do we always feel so busy? Despite the fact that we all feel like we're working harder and longer hours than ever before, sociologist John P. Robinson from the University of Maryland stresses that this is a form of widespread self-delusion. When studying the average number of hours on the job, he discovered that the numbers have either held steady or *decreased* for the 40 years! His findings show that we actually have more time for leisure than we did in the past.[1]

So, if we aren't working more hours but still feeling overworked, what is causing this feeling? It's likely the way we're spending our time, further proving that we need to get it together.

To me, getting it together at work means starting the workday with a plan, staying organized, and keeping myself focused and on task throughout the day. It means working *up* and not *out* (more on that in a bit), feeling accomplished at the end of the workday, and disconnecting from work once I get home. It also means that I am in control of my day through the different systems I have put into place to churn results.

And, that's exactly what we'll be discussing in these chapters. The tools that I will share in this chapter, which I call CIBP: calendar, inbox, bullet journal, and project management system, all help me to do my best work in a reasonable amount of time—and can help you do the same.

Let's jump right in!

# CALENDAR

Designate one place to put all of your commitments. Even if you have a planner, I'd recommend putting your appointments somewhere electronically. This allows you to access your calendar from anywhere.

When it comes to your calendar for work, I'm a believer in using compatible systems. Most people use either Outlook or Gmail for e-mail. Meaning that if you have Outlook for e-mail, use Outlook Calendar (Microsoft 365). If you have Gmail, use Google Calendar. I currently use Outlook Calendar—I've found that for me, it's better for business. For years, we used Google Calendar, but we felt like it was hard to synchronize with other businesses. In my line of work (marketing agency/lifestyle brand), I felt like more people were using Outlook, so I made the switch.

It doesn't matter which system you use, just use something! I used to think that I could remember everything. Guess what? I couldn't! Now, I've made up a rule that a commitment isn't final until it goes into the calendar. I'll discuss the downside of instant planning and saying yes to things without first checking in Chapter 8. But remember to always check your calendar before making a commitment and then lock it in!

When I put things in my work calendar, I always include the following:

- **Subject.** Name of the people on the call, company they are from (in parentheses), and reason for the call. If I'm going to be speaking with my team, I'll just put the word "team."
- **Location.** Conference line number, my cell phone (if they are calling me directly), our office address, or the address of where the meeting is being held.
- **Start time/end time.** Pitch calls with an external company are set for 30 minutes, and internal calls, interviews, student calls, or internal meetings are 15 minutes. As I mentioned before, a goal of mine is keeping meetings to 15 minutes, but I don't want to make outside vendors feel rushed, so I'll keep the 30-minute duration, but privately, I'll time myself!
- **Body of the calendar invite.** Agenda, directions (when needed), notes, and necessary attachments that pertain to the meeting. Sometimes, I'll even attach the e-mail correspondence so that I can quickly reference the e-mail chain that led to setting up the meeting.

In addition to utilizing the above functions of the calendar, here are some additional tips for managing your work calendar:

- If I'm putting a meeting in the calendar, I'll check the distance (overestimate it by 30 minutes since traffic is terrible) and put a time to leave in my calendar as well.

- If the call is reoccurring or something that needs to be followed up on a reoccurring basis, I'll immediately make it a reoccurring meeting so I don't forget.
- Always double-check to make sure all appointments appear on the calendar where they should. I've had issues with this in the past, and it's not fun!
- I share my work calendar with several members of my team and my husband. I do this just in case they need to make plans on the spot and can't ask me first. This is also helpful in general when they need time with me or have a quick question.
- If an event is pending, I still put it in my calendar and mark as "Holding." If I don't, I'm likely to overbook.
- On Fridays, I evaluate how I spent my time that week. I review the Time Chart I created on the previous Friday and make sure my actions that week aligned with my plans. I summarize how I spent my time and compare this with how I said I want to be spending my time. Then, I plan next week and use the information I just gathered as necessary. Remember, this time is crucial because it's your way to align your schedule and priorities. This is an opportunity to take control of your time and spend it as you wish.

## The Importance of Fridays and Sundays

Fridays and Sundays are the best days of the week not only to review how your week went, but to set yourself up for success next week. My Fridays and Sundays are full of review and planning. Even if I do a solid review on a Friday, I always like to go over things on Sundays to make sure I'm set up for success.

First, I scroll up and down the calendar to make sure I don't have anything scheduled early in the morning or super late at night. I've missed stuff in the past from simply not scrolling through the whole page.

Next, I go through the items on the calendar. I accept anything that I haven't accepted, adjust the duration of appointments if necessary, add any team members who might be missing on a specific invite, and delete any canceled items.

If my schedule isn't working, I check for internal calls that I can easily move around. Because I don't like having small unnecessary gaps in my schedule, I make sure my calendar works for me.

Once my schedule is set, I review the Action Plans that I set up for reaching my YQMB. I ask myself, "When am I going to do what I need to do in order to accomplish my goals?" I'll create calendar invites for myself in order to accomplish these tasks and change my status to "busy." I also share these time slots with our assistant so she knows to leave those time slots free (meaning, I'll actually invite her to the "meeting").

Now that my schedule and YQMB goals for work are in the calendar for the week, I'll glance over the time pie chart (we are about to review this in the notebook section). If my schedule and priorities are not aligned, I adjust accordingly. If it's a super busy day and I can't fit something in, I'll block more time for it the following day. The schedule won't be perfect, but we can try to get it as close as possible.

# INBOX

Now, there is a school of thought that many follow (including my husband who's a big Gmail guy) that you don't delete anything from your inbox so that it's 100 percent search-friendly and you can find anything you need at any moment. I've looked at inboxes like this—and they look crazy! I definitely prefer a clean inbox. However, when I started this project, my inbox was at 7,771—argh! I knew I had to fix my e-mail problem not just for the time being, but for good. I immediately began researching.

First, I needed to clean out my e-mails, and then I needed to learn how to maintain the organized inbox. The goal was to be like my sister-in-law, with less than 100 e-mails always. I wanted my inbox to only include items that needed to be handled. Anything that's already been responded to should be filed away in a beautifully labeled folder. But how do you keep up with your inbox without spending all day on it?

When I finally sat down to clean out my inbox, I did an exercise. I went through e-mails for 30 minutes and then wrote down the three top e-mail requests that I get. For me, they were:

1. Student advice requests
2. Scheduling requests
3. Sales pitches

I immediately drafted three e-mail templates to respond to these types of e-mails that could be personalized quickly. Having these e-mail templates ready to go really helped me blast through my inbox.

Here's a list of the next steps that I took to clean out my crazy inbox:

First, I started sorting by "From" instead of by the date (what it's normally set to sort by). When I asked people about cleaning out my inbox, they suggested I sort by the "Importance" filter. When I tried that, a bunch of deleted meetings and old CPA tax requests popped up. These were e-mails that other people had marked as important, not me. For me, sorting by "From" was the most helpful, because I could file everything from one sender at the same time. For example, let's say I have 45 e-mails sitting in my inbox from Margie, our marketing manager. I can scroll down to Margie's name (on the "From" search), and I can glance over all of the e-mails (mostly old correspondence), see if there's anything new to handle, and then click on her name and file every e-mail she's sent me into an Assistant folder. This way, I'm clicking twice, instead of having to go through every single e-mail she's sent me.

Next, I started to mass delete as many items as possible. As I said above, I like to be able to mass delete e-mails from a specific sender. This is the only way to go through my e-mails quickly. Let's say Bank of America has sent me 50 spam e-mails. If I'm sorting by "From," they are all going to be in one collective place. I can simply click on the beginning of the category and press "Delete," and all those messages will disappear with one click.

Using e-mail folders to get organized has been crucial in getting my inbox together. I like having different e-mail folders for all our active clients. I also have a folder named Pitches where I put any pitch responses (rejections or random correspondence). This way, when I do my follow-ups, I simply open that folder and go down the list. If I had a folder for every client I've ever spoken to, the list of folders would go on for days and I'd never be able to keep up. Besides our active clients, every other folder is labeled by project type. For example, I have one named CPA, and any e-mails from my CPA's office get filed in that folder. Another folder is named Book, and I store any book-related correspondence there. I have a folder named Student E-mails where I put student advice requests. In general, I like keeping correspondence just in case there's any discrepancies or if I need to check on any specifics.

## Maintaining a Clean Inbox

E-mail is tricky. As I said, if you spend all day on e-mail answering other people's requests, you won't be able to stay on track and spend your time in the way you want—(on your YQMB and Time Chart). Earlier, when we set our time goals, we talked about e-mail and decided that on a good day you will spend less than two hours on e-mail. Now, with less than two hours per day on e-mail, how can you manage it effectively and keep an organized inbox?

Here are a few of my e-mail tips on how to maintain the organized inbox:

- Have specific times throughout the day when you are going to check your e-mail. Set a timer for 10 to 15 minutes and see what you can organize in that block of time.

- Look for any important client e-mails that need to be answered or handled first.
- Add any task requests to a project management system that is linked with your inbox (more on that soon).
- Don't just delete junk mail, but send it to the Block Sender category. The less junk in your inbox, the better.
- Immediately file or delete items that you are copied on but don't need to handle. A quick note on blogs or newsletters you subscribe to: keep your top five and purge the rest, and if you have an app for a certain company, keep the app and unsubscribe to the e-mail newsletter. (I love getting e-mail updates from Tone It Up, Kayak, and Tim Ferris's newsletter for business. Other than that, I delete it all!)
- Accept and send out calendar invites right away.
- If there's a student e-mail or something that I want to handle but know I won't have time for, I forward it to someone on my team who I know can handle it. If you can delegate, I suggest you do. And if you can't, flag it and create a new task for it in your project management system.
- Respond to what I'd call a "two-second response e-mail" (for example, anything I can respond to with a simple "Thanks!," "Sounds good!," "I've attached our media kit!," or "Send me times that work!," etc. ).
- Manage senders' expectations. Sending e-mails such as this go a long way: "I wanted to confirm that I got this e-mail and I'll definitely get back to you by Friday."

- If an e-mail requires a longer, thought-out response, leave it for later.
- If something needs to be handled by end of day (EOD), flag it so it sits on top of your inbox.
- If it's a task-related request (a client needs an invoice, a sales team member needs to review a proposal), block time in the calendar to meet with the person and discuss.
- When it comes to dealing with long e-mail chains, Sarah Boyd, founder of Simply, says she has a rule: "If you can't solve the issue with about two rounds of back-and-forth e-mails, just pick up the phone and call." This is much more efficient than relying on a ton of back-and-forth.
- Group e-mails by conversation so all e-mails in a chain appear together instead of taking up a ton of room in your inbox.
- When I interviewed YouTuber and content creator Brooke Miccio, she shared some e-mail organization tips. She uses Spark, an e-mail app for Mac users. She said it enables you to categorize and prioritize your inbox. For Brooke, she's able to easily prioritize items from school or for work by using the system.
- Sarah Boyd also mentioned a tool called Boomerang that helps you prioritize your inbox on Gmail so that important e-mails pop to the top of your inbox.

# NOTEBOOKS

If you follow my work, you know my belief about notebooks; they can change lives. When I'm feeling down, unorganized, and like I just can't get it right—a fresh notebook can fix everything. A notebook provides us an opportunity to create our plan and to set our goals.

## Planners

There's a large number of people who obsess over their planners to help them prioritize, organize, and maximize each day. While I certainly respect the planner mafia, this tool hasn't worked for me to date (I'll explain my system soon). But, for those of you who do love planners, here are a few tips from friends in this community.

One of our former campus ambassadors, Shanette Buford-Brazzell, is a manager at the United Way in Cleveland, Ohio. Shanette suggests using different colors for different activities. "I use color ink pens, Paper Mate Flair pens, or Sharpie pens to prioritize my to-do list and notes," she explains. Her color coding system is as follows: red for top priorities, blue for business- and organization-related tasks, purple for events, and green for other tasks. She also keeps a running personal and professional to-do list in her planner and updates it every Friday for the week ahead. In addition, she tries to limit her to-lists to no more than five items (something I've also recommended throughout the book).

Brooke Miccio says that the biggest perk of having a planner is the ability to visualize your calendar on a monthly and weekly basis. Brooke also uses highlighters to call attention to her biggest priorities in her planner.

Another YouTuber, Belinda Selene, who has one of the most viewed videos on planners, explains that the more interactive you get with your planner (decorating it with pens, stickers, and fun tape), the more you'll use it. Check out her channel to see a bunch of fun techniques to decorate your own planner!

I also reviewed two very popular planners last year, the Erin Condren LifePlanner and the Lilly Pulitzer Agenda. They were reasonably priced, had tons of room for note-taking, and were filled with fun colors. To check out my full review, watch my YouTube video on @InternQueen called "Finding the Perfect Planner + Giveaway."

## Bullet Journal

As I mentioned earlier, I'm not a fan of traditional planners, but I am a huge fan of personalizing notebooks to work for you. When I'm feeling stressed, busy, or that I don't have it together, I get a fresh notebook, open it up, and find solace in the blank pages. It feels like a symbol of new beginnings.

I've combined this love for fresh notebooks, to-do lists, planners, and goals in one place: my DIY Bullet Journal.

If you aren't familiar with bullet journaling, it's a great way to customize your own perfect planner. BulletJournal .com describes bullet journaling as a "customizable system and forgiving organization system. It can be your to-do list, sketchbook, notebook, and diary, but most likely it will be all of the above. It will teach you to do more with less."

When people research bullet journaling, they tend to be intimidated by the notebooks filled with Instagram-worthy block letters and calligraphy on Pinterest. Don't let this be you! I'll tell you now, I definitely don't have pretty handwriting, but this is the only planner that works for me.

Bullet journaling is supposed to be adjusted to what works best for you, so I've created a twist on the traditional bullet journal and created something that works perfectly for me.

Before I describe what's in my bullet journal, I want to mention that I do like to keep it simple. I feel that once you have too many boxes, charts, and graphs to fill out, it becomes a planner that you'll never keep up with. My goal is to make my bullet journal last for an entire quarter so that I only need four of them each year. This reminds me to write small, never leave a page blank, and use my space wisely. My bullet journal also helps me keep all of my to-do lists in one place. If you have notes on various Post-its, apps on your phone, and random pieces of paper, you might find yourself having a hard time trying to find what you're looking for. This journal keeps everything organized and in once place for you for quick and easy reference.

Without further ado, here's what you'll find in my bullet journal (photos included!).

### *Restate Goals*

If I'm going to use this bullet journal every day, I need to make sure my goals are the first thing I see. The first three pages are dedicated to each of my goals. On each page, I restate my YQMB, Action Plan, and where I should be after every two weeks of that month. At the bottom, I make a thermometer that shows how close or far away I am from reaching that goal. I'm shade this in every two weeks as I get closer to my goal for the quarter. You can see my goals here:

## Time Pie Graph

Next, I take out the time pie graph we created in Chapter 4. I draw this into page 4 of my bullet journal as a visual representation about how I want to be spending my time each week. I use a coffee mug to make the circle! You can see a photo from my bullet journal below. Follow my example to create your own!

It's important to have this at the front of my notebook so I can review it daily. When you aren't sure that you are spending your time in the right way, use this pie graph and determine what needs to change.

## Communication Log

On page 5 I keep a communication log to track of how often
keep in touch with the people I have strong relationships with
inside and outside of the office. First I write the initials of my
team members, clients, mentors, friends, and family members.
Next, I divide up the names by four categories: daily, weekly,
monthly, and quarterly. I make a dot by each person's name
every time I speak to them in the corresponding column. This
is an easy and effective way to see whom I'm communicating
with either too frequently or not enough. The next time I need
a new bullet journal (because I've run out of pages), I restart
this chart. You can see my communications chart below:

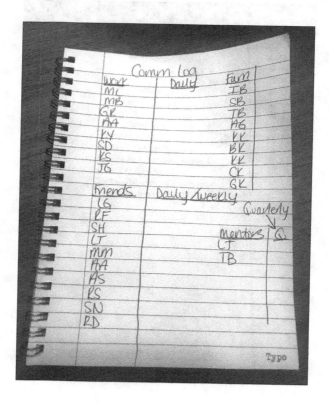

## Happiness Page

Page 6 of my bullet journal is always my happiness page. I like to use this page to keep track of when I feel happy or have a really great day. Anything I've done that day to contribute to my mood gets put on the list. The idea here is that when I'm feeling down, I can review this list and do one of those things that made me happy. For example, yesterday I woke up early and had a full hour to myself before I had to dive into the workday, which was relaxing and made me feel refreshed. I added this to the happiness page.

## *Task Lists*

The rest of the notebook is made up of to-do lists and notes
I'm a big believer in crossing out items when they are done
so my to-do lists aren't too pretty (but, like I said earlier, tha
isn't the point of a bullet journal!). I know this may seem like a
really short customized bullet journal, but I found that wher
you overcomplicate it, you can't realistically keep up with it.

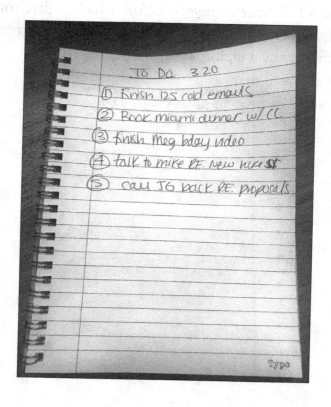

# PROJECT MANAGEMENT SYSTEM

here are a ton of project management systems out there, and ver the past few years, we've used a lot of them for different easons (including Basecamp, Trello, Freshsales, Salesforce, nd Jira). Today, we are using a system called Wrike. We do ay for it (a monthly fee per user), but there are free trials and different versions of the system.

When we started looking for a project management sys-tem, we decided we wanted something similar to what we've used in the past but also fresh and new. I didn't want any-thing with too many bells and whistles, and I wanted it to be simple and not too technical. We first made a list of what we needed the project management tool to have, which included the ability to:

- Assign tasks to different people
- Organize our task list so we weren't relying on multiple Google Docs
- Mark tasks as complete
- Share across all team members
- Sort task lists by the deadlines
- See the progress of a campaign from start to finish (almost like a Gantt chart)
- Have a bird's-eye view of the business
- Access from our phones and computers (for when I'm traveling).

As my company has grown, I've learned that you need a system to implement a system. While this may sound silly, it's really true. If you are going to ask other team members

to adapt to new systems and tools, there must be a proces
Today, we have an outlined process for rolling out anythin
new (systems, procedures, and policies). You can read mor
about this on my websites! Before you decide to roll out, pur
chase, or use a new project management system for yoursel
or for your team, ask yourself these questions and take the
answers to all of the different product demos:

- Why do I need this system? What problem am I trying
  to solve?
- Have I tested this system (that I want to use) and at
  least two others?
- Before I sign up or pay for this, have I tried all the
  demos and training videos provided? (If you are going
  to use something, you might as well take advantage of
  the resources!)
- Have I researched the pricing (against at least two
  other competitors), and is it reasonable? Have I
  negotiated?
- Do I have the necessary parties' signatures to sign off
  on this purchase?
- When can I create a learning system so that all of our
  team members are using this in the same way?

When using a project management system, the key is com-
mitting to it. If you are going to use it properly, everyone at
the company (even the execs at the top) need to use it for
projects on a daily basis.

## Cloud-Based File Storage System

Instead of saving things to your desktop or computer, I suggest using a cloud-based file storage system like Dropbox, Google Drive, or OneDrive where you can easily save and share files. You can access these files from anywhere, use the apps on your phone, and easily share these files and documents with collaborators.

If you decide to use one of these systems, I highly suggest you define exactly how you plan to use each. For example, our team tends to use Google Docs for documents and Dropbox for photos. It's also crucial to keep these storage systems organized—otherwise, they start to resemble messy inboxes. Whenever you are done with a document and don't need to save it, delete it. Whenever you upload something, be sure to name it clearly and put it in the proper folder. If you decide to upload personal photos to this system, make sure they aren't shared with your team. Also, if you have clients with an "I want to know everything" mentality, you can share your docs or photos with them directly and they can see updates in real time.

I'm a big believer in not only tracking your work but also utilizing tools that help you do the work more efficiently—and thanks to all of the tools you are now working with, you will be set up for success.

In the next chapter, we will learn how to design your success at work—and I'm confident that's possible.

# Chapter 6

# HOW TO GET GREAT WORK DONE

've talked about goal-setting and the tools you need to be successful at work. I've also told you how to create a bullet journal and roll out new systems. Next, I'd like to focus on how to ensure that you are actually getting great work done.

## CREATING A DISTRACTION-FREE WORK ZONE

Here at the Intern Queen office, we used to have an employee who was constantly distracted. Every time I'd look up, she was moving around the office. She was outside one second, then inside the next. Then she was off to get water, clean her desk, eat a snack, send a text, or water a desk plant. I rarely saw her working. I told her that in our small but always busy company, she needed to find a way to focus.

As someone who's also had issues being able to focus, I fe
for her. It's hard to find your focus zone, disregard everythir
happening around you, and just get your work done. Befor
getting it together, I was constantly distracted. I would si
down to work on this book, and it would take me hours to ge
through a handful of pages. Why? Because my phone woulc
ring, I'd get a text, I'd get an e-mail, I'd have someone ask me
a question, I'd need to use the restroom, my computer woulc
die, I'd need to get more water, I'd need a fresh coffee—the
list went on and on. Before I knew it, not only was I avoiding
the workload in front of me, but I was scrolling on a stranger's
Instagram page admiring her winter boots. The next thing I
know, I'm ordering the winter boots from Nordstrom.com—
clearly, not what I was trying to accomplish. This was exactly
the opposite of what I was trying to do. The result of this constant distraction zone was simple: nothing was achieved. On
top of that, I was frustrated and mad at myself, and felt unca-
pable of finding a distraction-free zone.

And while distractions aren't always a bad thing, they
keep you from getting your work done. A distraction could
be a text from your mom or a call from your best friend.
These are great people—whom you certainly want to connect
with—but connecting with them at that instance will likely
put you behind. Also, creating a distraction-free zone isn't
specific or unique to project-based work. Oftentimes to get
any sort of real work done, we need to create our own caves
and simply disconnect.

# FIND YOUR FOCUS

Today, after many trials and tribulations, I'm excited to report that I'm able to create that distraction-free zone and get work done. After so many internal arguments, I finally told myself, that I needed to grow up, focus, and figure it out. When I interviewed Laura Vanderkam, she said something that really stuck with me: "If you want to get it done, you'll get it done." She was right. These were my projects that I was passionate about, and I did want to get them done. And let's be honest, no one was going to do them for me. I had to find a way. I had to prove (first, to myself) that it was possible to get things done in a world full of cell phone notifications and 24-hour communication. It took time, but here's how I finally got myself focused.

## Block Time on Your Calendar

Remember when I talked about locking your day? Make sure to block time in the calendar to focus on any projects you might have. Yesterday, one of our team members was having a hard time crossing items off her to-do list because she kept getting distracted. I told her she needed to put the tasks in her calendar—it was the only way to get them done. She did this and, sure enough, it enabled her to focus and complete the tasks.

## Music Playlist—Lunch Time

As I mentioned, I go to town with my e-mails over lunch. Usually, it's sales e-mails so I'm in the mood for music that will get me in the right mindset to pitch myself and the brand. As you'll find, I have a very eclectic taste in music and while I'm working I can do fast music or slow music, the key is continuously switching it up:

**Rise Up**
*Audra Day*

**Time to Say Goodbye**
*Sarah Brightman*

**Side to Side**
*Ariana Grande*

**Focus**
*Ariana Grande*

**I Want It That Way**
*Backstreet Boys*

**Formation**
*Beyonce*

**Waiting for a Star to Fall**
*Boy Meets Girl*

**Shape of You**
*Ed Sheeran*

**Love Yourself**
*Justin Bieber*

**Sorry**
*Justin Bieber*

**Despacito**
*Luis Fonsi and Daddy Yankee
featuring Justin Bieber*

**Bad Things**
*Machine Gun Kelly and
Camila Cabello*

**Black Widow**
*Iggy Izalea featuring Rita Ora*

**Can't Stop This Feeling**
*Justin Timberlake*

**The Champion**
*Carrie Underwood featuring
Ludacris*

**Perfect**
*Ed Sheeran*

**Born This Way**
*Gaga*

**Let It Go**
*James Bay*

**Like I'm Gonna Lose You**
*Meghan Trainor*

**Fight Song**
*Rachel Platten*

## Use Headphones

For the holidays, I asked for nice headphones. My friend Rachel Doyle, founder and former CEO of GlamourGals, had a rose gold pair that I absolutely loved. The initial purpose of the headphones was for the gym, as I thought they'd keep me motivated. I didn't realize they'd also help me stay focused at the office. Just the act of putting on the headphones was a signal to my team that I was trying to focus, and I found team members were more likely to let me alone (and let me do my thing). I'm a person that can work with music and sometimes does better with music playing.

## Remove Distractions

When I have a writing project to finish, I do a few different things to remove distractions. First, I disconnect the Wi-Fi on my computer. Second, I close all tabs and programs that aren't being used. Third, I flip my phone over (it's actually turned over as I write this). Phones, open tabs, and Wi-Fi provide more distractions than we realize (news alerts, social media pings, e-mails, texts, shopping discounts, and more), so removing them whenever possible helps me create a space where I can really focus.

## Alert Those Around You

When I'm going into my distraction-free zone, I try to alert people to manage their expectations. At work, we all use Skype or Slack to communicate. I'll leave the team a message

before closing out of the program for a few hours. I typically
include a note such as "Hi all, I'm going into my writing cave
for a bit. I'll be back on in two hours. Please make a list of any
questions and I'll get back to you soon!" I'll do the same thing
with any friends or family members who I know might be
trying to get in touch over the next few hours. I'll send them
a text to say, "Doing work at coffee shop for a bit. Call you
after!" It's important to remember to be back when you say
you'll be back, too. I'll talk more about managing friends and
family expectations in Chapter 8.

## Turn People Away

Throughout this book, I have mentioned and will continue to
mention the importance of establishing boundaries. When
you need to focus, you need to set boundaries with the people
around you, especially those who are likely to cause a distraction. When you are in focus mode and someone asks you a
favor, only agree if it works on your timeline. You can say something along the lines of "I'd love to help. I'm working on a project
until 1 p.m. Let's set up a time to meet after that," which estab-
lishes a boundary and is professional. In the first chapter of the
book, I discussed taking yourself seriously and you advocating
for yourself. If you don't set a boundary here, who will?

## Utilize Your Notebook for Unrelated Ideas

If I have an idea that's not related to the project that I'm
working on during focus time, I make a note of it in my bullet
journal so it can be dealt with post–focus zone.

## Hydrate

Having a cup of coffee next to me really gets me into the zone. It's my motivation in a cup! Because I always make sure I have everything I need when I get settled in for a project, water and a cup of coffee are always nearby. Whatever your drink of choice (coconut water, sparkling water, or hot tea), have it nearby!

## Plan Your Timing

Before you get started, plan how long you are going to focus. Give yourself a time goal before you get started, and try not to work blindly (with no time and goal in place). Speaking of time goals, are you familiar with the Pomodoro Technique for work productivity and focus? As I was researching, I came across this time management method, and there is tons of research to prove its effectiveness. This method requires you to break your workday into 25-minute chunks separated by 5-minute breaks. After a few of these chunks of time, you take a longer break of 15 to 20 minutes. It's suggested that you use a timer to track these 25-minute blocks of time (you can even use this timer on your computer: https://tomato-timer.com/). The idea is that you are not only giving yourself a set time to work on a specific task, but you are also taking enough breaks to avoid burnout.[1]

## Determine When You're Most Productive

For me, early mornings are the most productive part of my day. Knowing when you're most productive and planning around it will set you up for success. Let me explain with an example. Today, I had to work from San Diego, which is about a two-hour drive from where I live in LA. My husband and I debated when to drive down (at night/post-traffic or super early in the morning/before work). Because I had a project to work on and I knew I'd be more productive in the morning, we decided to drive down late at night so that I could work in the morning. I felt empowered by this decision because it not only reflected my goals but was proof that I knew myself well enough to make the best decision for me. Now that I know mornings are best (for me), I try to wake up early to accomplish my goals and get into my distraction-free zone, no matter where I am.

## Turn Preventing Distractions into an Art Form

Test yourself. Yes, you should be able to create a distraction-free zone when it's early in the morning, but technically, you should also be able to do so at any time.

In order to create your distraction-free zone at the drop of a hat, you must know what tools you need (example: my Beats headphones) and you must know what actions you need to take to make this work (example: turning my phone upside down or placing it across the room). For me, if I know I have to focus on a big writing project at 2 p.m., I need to make sure I have my headphones and a fresh iced coffee ready and alert the people around me that I'm going into "the zone."

Being able to create this space for yourself is a sign that you are starting to really take control of your own time and

he way you spend it. This is a big step in your journey to get
t together!

## Think About the *Why*

Sometimes we are so wrapped up in productivity, to-do lists,
and getting things done that we forget about the *why*. Why
are we working on this project in the first place? Why did we
originally want to work on this project? Thinking back can
sometimes remotivate you to do great work.

When I take a breath and ask myself *why* I do what I do,
the answer is something like this: I started my business to
be the career resource I never had. My *why* is to help people
make the most of their career while also having fun and feeling inspired. When I get caught up in a crazy deadline or an
event that didn't go my way, I remind myself that I'm not in
it for the deadlines or the events (yes, they come with the ter-
ritory), but at the end of the day I'm trying my best to help
others succeed.

# PRIORITIZE

It wasn't until recently that I came to understand how awful
I was at prioritizing. I truly believed everything was important, and this set a bad precedent for myself and my team.
If I can't clearly articulate what to work on first, how will
my team be able to do so? Over the past year, I've learned to

prioritize based on urgency, deadlines, consequences, compli cations, and processes.

I do this by constantly looking at my to-do list (of no more than five items) and asking myself these five questions:

1. Which projects are **urgent** vs. important?
2. What tasks have an immediate **deadline**?
3. Which project comes with the biggest **consequence** if not handled today?
4. Which task is the most **complex**?
5. Which task has a long **process**?

If you ask yourself these questions, you'll find that your starting point will be clear. Let's work through each a bit more.

## Urgency

I follow the mantra of Sarah Knight, author of *Get Your Sh*t Together*, who stresses the need to prioritize based on urgency. Something that is urgent is time sensitive, is pressing, or requires immediate attention. Don't get lost in the urgent versus important battle. Many things can be important, but what is urgent?

## Deadline

Another part of this puzzle is figuring out how to prioritize multiple projects when none of them are urgent. The easiest solution: do them in order of when they are due. What is the deadline for each project? Prioritize by the deadline or date deliverables are due!

## Consequence

A lot of times, it won't be that easy to prioritize. But one question to consider is: Which project has the biggest consequence if not handled properly? Unfortunately, if you have one difficult client and one amazing client, oftentimes the difficult one is prioritized because you don't want to deal with the consequences of that client being upset.

## Complexity

Another way to determine where to focus your attention first is by following my motto of doing the task you want to avoid first. This not only gets a complicated task off your desk at the start of the day, but it makes you feel accomplished right off the bat. The better you feel about yourself and your performance during the day, the better you'll do all around.

Remember, not every task is created equal. Just because something is easy to complete doesn't make it urgent or any sort of priority. Adam Braun says, "Don't spend time on the small wins that just make you feel good about yourself, it's about knowing what really moves the needle."

## Process

And finally, you need to determine which item requires a response before proceeding. Let's say you are trying to organize a conference call for 10 people. The steps you'll need to take to complete the task are as follows:

1. Determine everyone's availability.

**2.** Once you get the availability, send out a calendar invite to confirm.

With these "stop and wait" tasks, it's always nice to get as fa as you can with the task and then circle back toward the en of the day to complete it. First thing, I may take step one so that I can follow up later in the day if I don't hear back and focus on completing the task by the end of the day.

## SHUT UP AND WORK

I have a philosophy I like to live by, and it's called "shut up and work." While it may sound harsh, it basically means that at some point, we must put our heads down and just get things done. One of my biggest pet peeves is when people talk about things but don't do them. It's easy to talk about ideas, but it's much harder to execute and put them into action. If you catch yourself chatting about work but not actually doing it, create that focus zone and get ready to shut up and work!

## HOLD YOURSELF ACCOUNTABLE

Not only do you have to be your own advocate, but you also have to you hold yourself accountable. You must take yourself seriously. Now, I say that with caution because I've also seen people take themselves so seriously that it fuels the busy

cle (I discuss how busy I am, so you discuss how busy you
e, and now we're both in a cycle of proving our worth and
:lf-importance based on busyness). There must be a balance.
art of holding yourself accountable is understanding the
.sk or consequence. What could happen if you don't accom-
lish your goal?

One of the consequences that I experience when I don't
.old myself accountable is personal frustration. I hate feeling
ike I didn't accomplish anything at the end of the workday. I
.ate asking myself, "What did I even do today?" after a long
lay of work.

I also try to avoid the domino effect. This is when you
don't get your work done, so you move the task to the next
day. While this may not seem important at the time, it could
turn into a habit that messes up your plan for the next day
and the day after that and the day after that.

We see this happen in our office frequently when small
projects are overlooked and pushed. This goes back to setting
practical goals. You must not only give yourself more than
enough time to achieve those goals, but you also have to
schedule time to work on them throughout your day.

## WORK *UP* NOT *OUT*

Another workplace goal of mine is to work *up* and not *out*.
Working *up* means that I'm growing the business. It's spending my time signing new clients, working directly on sales,
implementing new procedures for efficiencies, and working

on new growth strategies. Working *out* is doing things just t
do them. As Tim Ferris says in his famous book *The 4-Hou*
*Workweek*, "doing something unimportant well does no
make it important." He also says, "Requiring a lot of time doe
not make a task important." You have to focus on the proj
ects that help you grow, not just put more work on your plate
Stop filling your days with "feelings" chats, e-mail responses
and busy tasks. These decision will move you laterally across
instead of vertically up the ladder.

I'll give you an example. I looked at my calendar the other
day and was stressed. There was hardly any time to schedule
what I needed to do (which included sending out new business
pitches and working on my book). So, I analyzed the value of
what was on my calendar. There were a few sales calls (that I
needed to take) and then a 1.5-hour block of two podcasts. I
looked up the podcasts, and they were student podcasts that
didn't have a huge following. While I'm more than happy to
do things like this, this specific day required me to prioritize. I asked myself, "Will these podcasts help me grow my
brand?" The answer was no, probably not, so I rescheduled
both podcasts for a month later when I knew things wouldn't
be as crazy and made time for what I needed to do.

I challenge you to look at your day and calendar the same
way. Which items enable you to work *up*, and which tasks are
an example of you working *out*? What are you doing just for
the sake of doing it? Ask yourself, "Is that activity helping me
reach my goals for growth?"

# STOP WORKING FOR THE SAKE OF WORKING

ome people sit at work late at night or come in early just to t there. They may be on Facebook or talking to a friend, but their mind, they think they're "working" because they are hysically at work. They are lying to themselves.

Stop working blindly, and stop spending hours on end taring at your inbox and waiting for another e-mail. Instead, vork strategically, work for a purpose, focus on your goals, and check things off your to-do list.

Some people also fall into the trap of thinking that when they make a mistake at work, they have to make up for it with extra hours in the office. Working longer hours typically isn't the solution. Instead, it's working smarter, not harder and identifying the problem so you can find a productive solution. Don't work just to work. Come up with a strategy or else it just leads to more chaos. When you are in a moment of frustration, take a moment to disconnect from it and come back with a clean slate and a new plan.

# WORK FOR RESULTS

In addition to not working blindly, I want to remind you that your work should yield results. If you are churning out the work but not getting the desired results, you should reconsider your strategy and potentially switch it up. You can work

until you are blue in the face, but if you aren't getting resul
what's the point?

When I hire people to work at my company, I look for pe
ple who understand how to be results-oriented. In fact, v
just had a situation with this last night. We have a client wh
hired us to throw shopping parties at its retail locations wit
our campus reps. Each party was supposed to have a min
mum of 20 attendees. My team worked hard behind the scene
to recruit, train, and hire the students. They monitored th
students as they promoted the events. At last night's even
only nine people showed up. This was extremely disappoint
ing as I knew my team put in a lot of work. The client didn'
physically see my team working, and from their perspective
they just saw low attendance at an event. I explained to my
team that in the client's eyes it really didn't matter how many
hours they worked on the program, the result was bad. Until
we can learn to be results-oriented, we cannot be effective.
Again, it's the result that matters, not the amount of work
that was put in.

# USE PDDS TO HELP YOU MEET DEADLINES

What's a PDD? you may ask. It's what I call a pre-due date.
This is an internal due date to ensure that you reach a deadline in a timely manner. You must make pre-due dates for
external deadlines to ensure success. Deadlines are always
assigned to projects (even if they are internal), so with every

adline we should also create a PDD to ensure that we reach ur goals. If you don't have a pre-due date you risk the typal "dog ate my homework" situation, a stressful planning hedule, or even completely missing the deadline. If something has a Friday deadline, the PDD should be two full days efore: Tuesday. This eliminates last-minute stress and gives ou extra time that you will be grateful for later. At Intern Queen, we utilize our project management system (Wrike) to et our PDDs and CDDs (client due dates).

Take hitting deadlines seriously. Josh Notes, energy executive efficiency and renewable energy systems expert, suggests pretending that you are going on vacation the day after the deadline. If you need to hustle to finish the project to get everything done and go off the grid for a while, you'll get out of your own way.

## TRIM THE INEFFICIENCIES

At work, I'm constantly searching for inefficiencies, processes that don't make sense, and opportunities or learning moments where our team can improve. I suggest that you always stay on the lookout for these, and when problems arise, look at the bigger picture solution instead of the "quick fix." A few months back, I was in a meeting and made a bunch of notes on paper and then had to spend 15 minutes translating what I had written. I could have just grabbed a computer, taken the notes in a Word doc, cleaned up the doc after the meeting, and sent it out right after. In contrast, today I was

in a meeting and had Wrike (our project management too
open the entire time. I took my notes directly on Wrike
create not only a call recap, but a task list based on every no
from the call. Now that is progress!

# KEEP LEARNING FOR PERSONAL GROWTH AT WORK

A good worker is inspired, motivated, and passionate about
his or her craft. Keep yourself engaged and always learning.
Don't forget the resources that are in front of you. Want to
learn about social media techniques? Ask the social media
director to coffee. Want to learn more about the marketing
side of the business? Take the marketing director to lunch.
Use your resources internally.

Don't forget about the countless external resources too.
Today's business world means access to continued learning
classes, workshops, virtual seminars, and more. These not
only help you better understand something you want to learn
more about but also show initiative and a unique passion for
learning—which employers notice.

## Podcasts

When I spoke to Adam Braun, founder of Pencils of Promise and cofounder of MissionU, he couldn't stop raving about podcasts. When it comes to personal growth and development, podcasts are his favorite. Pull out your phone and bring up your podcasts app because you are going to want to subscribe to Adam's favorite podcasts:

- The Moth (storytelling)
- 99% Invisible
- Radiolab
- School of Greatness with Lewis Howes (one of Braun's friends)
- Rich Roll
- NPR's *How I Built This with Guy Raz*
- WorkLife with Adam Grant

# SAY THANK YOU (ALWAYS)

My friend Rachel, founder of GlamourGals, always stresses the importance of saying thank you. She's really inspired me to check myself when it comes to how much I'm thanking the people around me. In fact, because of Rachel, I've implemented a new thank you note system that I'd like to share with you. I'm going to send out two thank you notes every week. As I'm writing this, I'm already brainstorming to whom I'm going to send thank you notes to this week. I challenge you to do the same!

# HAVE EFFICIENT MEETINGS

We have six rules for meetings at Intern Queen, and I recommend you follow them as well.

1. **Agendas are required.** Meetings don't happen without agendas—especially internal meetings. If you don't have an agenda, you shouldn't be meeting with your colleagues. An agenda requires that you think before you meet, and writing down everything you need to cover helps you stay on track so that you cover everything of importance. I swear by agendas—they can take hours off meetings!

2. **No interruptions are allowed.** If you have questions, write them down and ask them at the end. We used to allow people to interrupt and ask questions during meetings, but it created a ton of back-and-forth, and never-ending meetings. Also, the question might be answered as the meeting goes on. Our new rule is once the leader is done going through all important updates and items, anyone is free to ask questions. Everyone is also reminded of the time. For example, the meeting leader might say, "All right. Well, it's 5:15 and we have 15 more minutes left. Does anyone have any questions, comments, or ideas they want to bring up?" If you know people may drag the conversation along, you could also add, "If we could keep our questions and ideas to about one or two minutes each, that would be great!" This is key as people tend to go on forever listing ideas if they have no time expectation set.

3. **Aim for 15-minute meetings.** Thirty-minute meetings don't typically last that long. Fifteen minutes is plenty of time for an efficient meeting. When it's time for me to pitch my brand to a company, I try to keep it under three minutes so I can keep the meeting moving. Focus on the important stuff, and keep it moving. You want to hit your buzzwords, and then let them ask questions.

4. **Include the agenda in the calendar invite.** I mentioned this earlier in the calendar section. I like to have the meeting agenda printed out before the call so I can write questions on it—ask at the end—cross them out—determine follow-up tasks—and move on. If we have a meeting with an external client, we ideally send the client the agenda at least a few hours before. It's frustrating to get an agenda 10 seconds before a meeting starts.

5. **Make agendas at the beginning of the week for all calls.** I usually try to do these on Sunday nights so I don't have to worry about them. This way they are done and handled for the rest of the week.

6. **Give your full attention.** When I spoke to Adam Braun, he confessed that his team used to tell him he wasn't engaged enough in meetings because he was too busy or on his phone. Once he heard this feedback he changed things, and now, whenever he's in a meeting his phone is down and laptop is closed. "You end up finding the time to clear those e-mails," he says, "you don't need to focus on this during meetings."

# NETWORK INSIDE AND OUTSIDE OF WORK (WITHOUT DRIVING YOURSELF CRAZY!)

Most people do what I call H/F networking or "hired and fired" networking. This means that you are consumed with networking only when you want to be hired or just got fired. To see the true value of networking, you must be consistent, thinking about it at all times, and (this is the hardest part) *while* you have a job.

## Networking Internally

At your current job, I recommend building below-the-surface relationships with the people around you. I can't believe how many people sit right next to each other every day at work for years but have never grabbed a cup of coffee together and don't know where the other is from or what their background is. People who develop deeper connections can work more successfully together, and because of this, we now have a mandatory policy for interns around this idea. They must grab a cup of coffee (the company pays) with every single team member before the end of their internship. We're implementing this for new team members as well.

Don't know what to ask coworkers? Sick of the awkward silence? Here are some conversation starters:

- Where are you from?
- Where did you go to school?
- Does your family live in the area?

- What do you normally do after work?
- What are your favorite restaurants in the area?
- Are you a morning person? What time do you usually get up to start your day?
- What's your ideal weekend? What are you usually up to on the weekends?

## Networking with Mentors

A few months back, I had a catch-up meeting with a mentor of mine in NYC who runs a big blogger/talent business. We had a good meeting, and I even felt like she opened up to me about things she was dealing with and feeling at work (which is always a great turning point in a mentor/mentee relationship), but I did feel like it got off track. Here's what I should have done better and what you should consider doing in a catch-up meeting:

- **Have five questions prepared.** Even though you might be meeting with someone who is more of a "friend" than a "mentor," the person will still have insights and advice that can help you! Whenever I walk into a meeting with a mentor, I like to ask myself, "What do you want to know from this person? What's a problem you are having where she may be able to help you find a solution?"
- **Read up on the person.** Come to your meeting already aware of what's new with people or the company they work with. Check their LinkedIn and any social media where you are connected and be

aware of any clients they might be working with that you are interested in learning more about.

- **Keep your eye on the clock.** If there's a time you or the person you are meeting with needs to leave, be aware of this. Find a way to have a clock in your peripheral vision (if possible), so you can be sensitive of the time.
- **Clearly identify the action steps at the end of a meeting.** Sometimes when meeting with friends or mentors, you won't want to follow up because you "feel bad" or you don't want to bother the person. Establishing what you owe them and what you're hoping to get from them gets you both on the same page and doesn't waste anyone's time.
- **Send a thank you note immediately following the meeting.** A handwritten note is always a nice touch—and will not go unnoticed. As a bonus, you could also send a short e-mail after the meeting, but remember this should be a quick thank you, and if there are follow-ups for your mentor, they should be small.

## Networking Externally

We all get comfortable in our jobs and forget to network. It's understandable. But what happens when we need to move on or get laid off? You never know what's going to happen, so you should always be networking inside and outside of your business. And with that, make sure to keep your résumé updated. Should there be a meeting that you need to take, ou want to make sure you have your materials easily accessible. Also, make sure that your social networks are updated and appropriate. LinkedIn should always be updated with your accomplishments and most recent position.

My favorite way to network externally is by setting up informational interviews with people who have jobs that you admire or are curious about. You can try connecting with them on LinkedIn and sending a note with your connection request. Write a short note requesting a quick advice phone call or coffee meeting. If you can find people that you have connections in common with, or people who graduated from your college—even better!

Additionally, attend networking events. I know I want to go home at the end of the day and watch Netflix and eat just as much as the next person, but I recommend you attend at least one external networking event (within your industry) every month. These could be professional associations that you've joined, alumni events, or just random panels that you find on Eventbrite. When I go to these events, I don't let myself leave before I meet at least five different people and get their contact information. Also, if possible, I like to research who's going to be at these events ahead of time so I can pinpoint certain people. I'll look them up on LinkedIn so I know what they look like.

Make sure you bring business cards, or something of the sort to give to people at these meetings. Also, if there are cocktails involved, you must keep it together. I'd recommend no more than two cocktails and, of course, make sure you have the right transportation home. If you haven't eaten before the event (this happens a lot as events tend to be scheduled

after work), be extra careful. You are here to network, an
you don't want to embarrass yourself.

And my last piece of advice for external networking i
not to burn bridges. You want to have positive relationship
within your industry to make you a desirable job candidate. I
people think you have a bad attitude or might be difficult to
work with, they are less likely to want to hire you some day.
Remember, you never know whom you will be working with
or working for in the future.

# RECEIVE FEEDBACK GRACEFULLY

Whenever I think of feedback at work, I think about Tar-
get because the company is known for having what's called
a "feedback-driven culture" where everyone gets feedback all
the time—even the CEO! Feedback is good to get but isn't
always the easiest to receive. We can't improve without it.
Here are some tips to deal with getting feedback:

- Bring a pen and paper to take notes.
- Ask questions and ask for examples. Make sure you
  understand the feedback you are getting. In fact,
  you could reiterate the feedback just to make sure
  you are understanding it. If you don't understand
  the feedback, use it as an opportunity to ask specific
  questions to understand where the person is
  coming from.
- Ask for advice on how you can improve any issues.

- If you know the feedback session is happening, prep for it with any questions or uncertainties about your performance.
- Thank whoever delivered the feedback. Remember, the person didn't have to do that.
- Come up with a plan for the next day to show you were listening.
- Even if you are the CEO or don't agree with the feedback, take the time to listen and consider what you have heard. Thank the person for providing it and consider the fact that he or she may be onto something.
- Try not to be defensive or give a "trigger finger response." By this, I mean take a moment to soak in the feedback you are getting and consider it. You don't need to react right in that moment or even in that conversation. You can simply thank the person for the feedback and tell him or her you are going to process it and you'll circle back with any questions.

## BE SUCCESSFUL WORKING FROM HOME

Did you know that over 22 percent of adults worked from home in some capacity in 2016? That number is expected to increase, according to the American Time Use Survey put out by the US Department of Labor. Many people are finally getting the opportunity to work from home or start their own

businesses, so having the skills to stay focused at home
essential for success. (Also, if you are reading this and still i
school, studying is another form of working from home, s
you'll benefit from this advice too!)

When working from home, have a place where you ca
focus. You need to establish where in your home you wil
get things done. I do have an office room, but I rarely use i
because I find that I'm most productive in the parts of the
house that have the brightest lighting. They also make me the
happiest to work from.

In addition to having a designated space, be sure it
includes everything thing you need to get your work done.
You want to sit down and be ready to work. You don't want to
have to get up for water, coffee, pens, chargers, etc.

Finding your groove when you work from home can take
time (as you learned was the case for me in Chapter 2). Here
are a few lessons I learned throughout that process:

- **Take yourself seriously.** When you work at home,
  you can technically do whatever you want. If your cell
  phone rings with a personal call during the workday,
  you could answer it. No one will be looking over
  your shoulder to monitor your actions. Because of
  this, you'll be faced with great temptation. However,
  once you start to take yourself seriously, set your
  own boundaries, and ignore anything that stops
  you from being productive, you will start to see your
  productivity skyrocket.

- **Get dressed.** You don't have to wear a business suit, but do put on clothes that make you feel confident and professional. You don't want to turn into a house rat like I did and start to doubt yourself.
- **Build relationships beyond the screen.** Working from home can be lonely, so go out of your way to build beyond-the-screen relationships. Make it a point to have coffee meetings with local execs and entrepreneurs a few days per week.
- **Go outside.** I also found that it's important to take a walk during lunch or circle the block while on a call. Whatever it is, do something to get out of your house and away from your desk.
- **Break your day up.** If you are spending all day at home, you should go do something (even if it's just running a silly errand) after working hours. No one wants to be in the same place for too long.

When I spoke to Brooke Miccio, mega YouTuber and content creator, she mentioned how hard it can be for her to focus at home, so she'll often head to the campus library for the day to work. If you are distracted or cannot focus at home, you should leave and go somewhere else. The second I feel a lack of focus, I grab my stuff and leave almost immediately. I can't sit there "getting ready to get ready." I need to decide, move, and get my work done.

# TRAVEL AND WORK TIPS

I travel at least 14 days per month and have learned quite
bit on these trips. Here are some personal lessons I've learne
along the way so you too can keep it together on the road:

- **Prepare for plane rides.** Make sure your flight is in
  your calendar and that you know exactly what time
  to leave for the airport with some wiggle room, just in
  case. Choose a seat where you're most comfortable and
  have everything you need (tickets, passport, license,
  snacks, etc.). I try to bring healthy food with me on
  the plane so I can feel great while traveling and stay
  healthy.
- **Have backup boarding passes and itineraries.**
  Even though we're living in a mobile world, I believe in
  having a backup for everything. I like to print copies of
  my daily calendar while I'm traveling (with plane times
  and meeting directions) just in case anything happens
  to my phone on the go.
- **Plan until you can't.** Once I get to the airport, I am
  fully aware of my travel plans. I'm also fully aware
  that they could change at any moment, so I plan until
  I can't. I try to zone out and have a "go with the flow"
  attitude once I arrive at the airport. Once I'm at the
  airport, I've done all I can. The rest is up to the skies!

- **Make a plane plan.** How will you spend your time on the plane? If I'm traveling on the weekends or super late at night, I'll give myself a break and maybe even buy a magazine. But if I'm traveling early in the morning or during the workday, it's on! If I'm going to have more than an hour of uninterrupted work time, I want to take it. Whether I'm catching up on e-mails, writing e-mails, or working on projects or proposals, I set a plan before I take off. I also try not to overplan because turbulence scares me and causes me to close my computer.

- **Carry business cards.** Always have business cards with you as you never know whom you'll meet on the road. Take more than you think you might need—you always want to have extra instead of not enough.

- **Use a packing list.** Before you blindly start packing, write out a packing list. I write out all the days and what type of outfit I need for that day. You can see my system on the following page.

| Day | Event | Type of Outfit | Notes |
|---|---|---|---|
| Monday, March 12th | Breakfast Speech | Professional | *Black pants |
| Monday, March 12th | Driving 3 hours | Comfy Clothes | *Bring Sweatshirt/Chill |
| Monday, March 12th | Dinner Meeting | Professional (Denim Works) | *Dark Jeans |
| Monday, March 12th | Sleep | Comfy Clothes | |
| Monday, March 12th | Gym | Gym | |
| Tuesday, March 13th | Gym | Gym | |
| Tuesday, March 13th | Lunch Meeting | Professional | |
| Tuesday, March 13th | Travel Home | Comfy Clothes | |

| Types of Clothes | Number of Outfits Needed per Category |
|---|---|
| Professional | 3 |
| Comfy Clothes | 3 |
| Denim | 1 |
| Gym | 2 |

I use a makeshift double table here. First, I log by the type of outfit I need and then I total up at the bottom how many of each "type" of outfit I need to bring. I take the list into my closet where I pack!

- **Don't overpack.** Why lug around more stuff than necessary? Only pack the essentials. You'll be happy you did!
- **Work out on the road.** Plan workouts ahead of time. Look at pictures of the hotel gym on the hotel website and see what you'll have at your disposal. You could also find a class nearby if that's what you prefer.
- **Eat healthy on the road.** Packing snacks on trips is always a plus for me. Not only do I avoid boring plane food, but I stay healthy, too. I always pack nuts, fruit, dried mango, and granola bars. If you know you'll be going to dinners or lunches on your trip, take a look at the menu and get an idea of what you should eat beforehand. This will help you stay on track when you're away from home. If you have any say over where you eat, try to pick places with healthy options.
- **Get your hair styled.** Now, this is a luxury, but if you can swing it, getting a blowout or a haircut before a business trip is amazing. Not having to worry about your hair for two or three days on your trip is such a time-saver.
- **Enjoy.** Try to do one thing for you during business trips. Go to a great restaurant, eat dinner alone, take a bubble bath, or order takeout in bed. No matter what it is, just do something that you enjoy. If you don't break the work travel up with some fun time, it will get daunting. Give your mind a break! You deserve it.

• • •

I know I shared a lot of information, strategies, and tips this chapter, but remember all of this *can* be done, and th does work. I've seen it. The days when I can follow my ow advice, my day feels complete. I feel as if I'm floating throug the day, completing tasks, managing other people's expect tions, and getting great work done. It's such a stark contra to the days when you come home feeling like you worked al day but accomplished nothing. By slowly implement differ ent ideas that I've suggested on different days (and tryin; your own), you'll grow tremendously and feel in control o your life.

# Chapter 7

# SOCIAL MEDIA AND DISCONNECTION

G rowing up, I was the only one out of my friend group who had a computer in my room. These were the days of AIM, Yahoo, and AOL chat rooms. I didn't have social media, a cell phone, or e-mail. Back then, the only way to get a news update was to turn on the television or listen to the radio. Celebrity gossip sites were few and far between, you exchanged money at the bank or at an ATM, you phoned a restaurant to request delivery, and you shopped in-store at the mall. Facebook was not a thing. Texting was not a thing. E-mailing was not a thing. Jonathan Taylor Thomas? Totally a thing!

Today's world is much different. My phone currently has the following app "notifications":

- 57 e-mails
- 1 CNN
- 7 Instagram messages
- 1 TMZ update.
- 2 Venmo requests

- 1 Postmates update
- 1 Macy's ad
- 4 Facebook likes
- 1 Starbucks mobile update
- 1 Topshop update
- 1 *New York Times* update
- 1 *Hollywood Reporter* update
- 7 text messages

Clearly things have changed.

Our phones and computers capture our minds in an entirely new and immediate way. Communication channels often come with what feels like a sense of urgency to respond immediately. But if we were to stop and read every single comment, alert, notification, and message—how could anyone have enough time to reach their YQMB goals?

Social media alerts, unanswered communications, and outstanding messages don't make me feel like I have it together.

Influencer agency Mediakix conducted a study that says the average person will spend more than five years of his or her lifetime on social media.[1] Isn't that crazy? We must learn how to take back control of our time.

# DEFINE WHY

Defining the networks that I use and why I use them was my first step in mastering social media, and I encourage you to do the same.

Sometimes we get so caught up in our messages and posts that we forget our original intention for using that specific platform. Take a step back and ask yourself, "Why do I use this platform? What's my intention here?"

It's important to be aware that the reason you originally started using a certain network can change with time. For example, I used to rely on Facebook for my personal brand. These days, I only use Facebook to catch up with friends and family and see what they're up to. We put lots of our time and energy into these networks, so let's revisit the original intention and see if each network is still worth spending time on.

## A Look into My Motives

The following list details two reasons why I use each social network and how often. I included a blank form for you to fill out at the end of my list as well.

### Facebook (*Personal Account*)
- Reasons for use:
  - Stay connected to old friends
  - Stay connected to family members
- Frequency: Biweekly or monthly

### Facebook (*Business Account*)
- Reasons for use:
  - Stay connected to older and alumni networks
  - Post career content that might interest that audience
- Frequency: Weekly

### Network: Twitter
- Reasons for use:
  - Promote new internship listings and blogs from our site
  - Show readers my personality and real life
- Frequency: daily

### Pinterest
- Reasons for use:
  - Find aspirational images for work, outfit, deco, and photo ideas
  - Find brands that advertise to our network
- Frequency: Monthly

### LinkedIn
- Reasons for use:
  - Connect with people I admire
  - Continue a professional dialogue with my audience
- Frequency: Weekly

### Instagram
- Reasons for use:
  - Portray a certain aspirational lifestyle and bring brand to life through images
  - Recruit college women for campaigns
- Frequency: Daily

### YouTube

- Reasons for use:
  - Create unique video content that relates to, educates, or inspires my audience
  - Attract first-time and young users to our site (who will turn into college-aged users)
- Frequency: Weekly

• • •

Now that you have an idea of why I use each social media platform, try this exercise yourself. Remember to include your two main reasons for use

**Network:** _____

- Reasons for use:

  - _____

  - _____

- Frequency: _____

**Network:** _____

- Reasons for use:

  - _____

  - _____

- Frequency: _____

***Network:*** _____

- Reasons for use:

  ○ _____

  ○ _____

- Frequency: _____

***Network:*** _____

- Reasons for use:

  ○ _____

  ○ _____

- Frequency: _____

***Network:*** _____

- Reasons for use:

  ○ _____

  ○ _____

- Frequency: _____

# BENEFITS OF SOCIAL MEDIA

ocial media can be an asset and a positive experience for all,
f you use it correctly and are in control of your time. Below is
breakdown of some of the biggest benefits:

- **Staying connected** with friends/family and professionally with colleagues and contacts
- **Meeting** new people
- **Reconnecting** with old friends and colleagues
- **Getting inspired** with new ideas, quotes, products, services
- **Feedback** on personal or professional projects or work
- **Recommendations** on restaurants, babysitters, bars, housing—the works!
- **Creating** and promoting content
- **Engaging** with other people

# THE INSTAGRAM JEALOUSY THING

I remember being in the car with my best friend driving up to Lake Tahoe. I was trying to explain that I didn't like to look at Instagram at night. Sometimes I got jealous, envious, or insecure looking at other people's Instagram feeds and would have issues going to sleep. At first she laughed, thinking I sounded ridiculous. I shot the question back at her, "Is there anyone you look at who makes you feel that way?" She thought about it, "Wait! That *does* happen to me!" She went on to say that for her, it was about other moms who looked like they had all together. She said she would look at posts and ask herself "Am I doing enough?" I loved hearing her example and felt like even though one was work-related and the other wasn't, we found a great way to connect over a common fear. And if Meghan and I were feeling it—I imagined just how many young men and women were feeling that same way.

So, how do we stop that jealousy? Stop following people that you can't handle looking at. Really. I did it. I unfollowed all our competitors. If I want to evaluate what the competition is doing, I can easily go to their pages, but there's no need for that feed to pop up whenever it chooses and pop into my day at random times. Adam Braun says that he unfollowed almost everyone. He says that he follows a handful of people who are meaningful in his life, and because of the low number he follows, there are rarely new posts, making Instagram much more manageable. Here are the ways I avoid Insta-jealousy:

- **Stop scrolling at night.** Don't end your day looking at someone else. There's no way that can possibly be relaxing.
- **Limit the amount of scrolling** during the day. In Chapter 3 we spoke about time goals—try not to spend more than 5 to 15 minutes scrolling.
- **Unfollow people you don't want to see.** You don't need them popping up in your feed day and night.
- **Remind yourself, social media isn't "real."** If you wanted to get your hair and makeup done and hire a photographer, you could also take a beautiful lifestyle photo.

- **Avoid the comparison game.** Ashley Robertson (theteacherdiva.com) says she's very mindful about getting distracted by social media. She explains that it's so easy to play the comparison game that "over the last year, I've really focused on staying in my own lane and focusing on me." Brooke Miccio also echoes Ashley's advice. She says, "Naturally, I'm going to be compared to other YouTubers." She says she really tries not to get stuck thinking about that. She tries to focus on her strengths and what she is really good at—"I'm my own person with my own strengths and weaknesses," says Brooke (well said!).

- **Take a break.** You don't have to post every single day. In fact, Ashley Robertson, who has hundreds of thousands of followers, says that something that makes her different is she doesn't post every single day, and that's okay.

- **Put yourself in time-out.** Make sure you are using social media for the reasons you laid out previously. If you notice you aren't using social media the way you intended, make yourself disconnect. Social media is typically something we look at on our own, so we must police ourselves. Instead of blaming social media for "making us feel a certain way," if we can learn to control our actions and follow our intentions, there's hope for all of us.

# MANAGING YOUR TIME

Now that we've talked about which networks we use, how we use them, and the intent behind these channels, let's explore how to know the right amount of time to spend on each.

When I made my time goals in Chapter 4, you may have noticed that I added in 45 minutes (on average) per day for checking social. Forty-five minutes to scroll each day isn't a big number as most people like to scroll a few times per day. My recommendation here is pick three networks per day and spend 15 minutes total on each network. You can scroll through a lot of photos on Instagram in five minutes! You won't need more than that unless you're conducting a work assignment (and in that case, make sure you stay focused on the task at hand!).

If a specific platform needs to be checked daily (like Instagram for me), then add two other networks each day. For example, Monday, you can check Instagram, Facebook, and Twitter. On Tuesday, you switch out Twitter with You-Tube. On Wednesday, you spend most of your social time on LinkedIn. Whatever you decide, just remember to keep track of your time. You're likely already on your phone, so just set your timer before you scroll.

## Eliminate Instant Responses

The best way to handle all the notifications, messages, and interruptions is to take away the expectation of instant responses. You don't need to respond to social media

mments immediately. Instead, use the time that we just set
r each network to respond to any communications.

## treamline Responses

's also important to streamline your communication. It's
npossible to have several conversations in multiple places
nd remember to get back to everyone. I manage this by
lirecting all my communication to one place—e-mail. When
>eople message me on Facebook, Twitter, LinkedIn, or Ins-
:agram, I tell them to e-mail me. This allows everyone's
nformation to be in one "sortable" place.

## Create Five-Minute Strategies

Worried that 15 minutes isn't enough for you on each platform per day? Here are my five-minute strategies for each
social network.

### Facebook in Under Five Minutes

If I'm posting content, I might need the full five minutes, but
usually I can get through Facebook in under five minutes.
After logging on, I do the following, each in one minute:

1. Scroll through and like friends and family updates.
2. Look at the birthdays section to see if there's anyone I
   need to reach out to with a birthday message.
3. Comment on photos that require engagement.
4. Check and accept any new friend requests.
5. Read and respond to new messages.

### Instagram in Under Five Minutes

If I can regulate my Instagram scrolling to five minutes at time, I'm less likely to go down the rabbit hole. I sign on Instagram to do the following:

1. Scroll through posts of the people I follow. If I see something I love or that inspires me, I'll take a screenshot.
2. Check out the Explore page.
3. Edit and post something of my own with a great caption. (Pro tip: Think of captions as mini-blog posts for more user engagement. Lauryn Hock gave me that advice!)
4. Answer messages.
5. If I have time left, check Instagram analytics.

### Twitter in Under Five Minutes

I usually spend the least amount of time on Twitter and barely read my feed. I typically do the following:

1. Check messages and notifications.
2. Engage with users that messaged me or asked questions.
3. Retweet some of my favorite tweets about Intern Queen.
4. Scroll through the home page for interesting or sharable content.
5. Check if anyone who is verified interacted with me, and if so I tweet at them.

### nkedIn in Under Five Minutes

nkedIn is the one network where I wish I had a few more inutes but managed to figure it out. On LinkedIn, I do the llowing:

1. Check to see who has viewed my profile lately.
2. Research and reach out to anyone who viewed my profile and sounds interesting.
3. Check my messages and respond.
4. Check my notifications. I like looking at the "new job announcements." I'll reach out to people and say "congrats" if I have time.
5. Check the activity on my posts. I take notice of which content people seem to be interacting with the most, and I'll share anything that's new or inspiring.

# MANAGING ALL OTHER NOTIFICATIONS

When we think about all the notifications and alerts coming from our devices, social media is a huge piece of it, but what about texts and app notifications?

Here are some basic rules for texting and apps:

- Texting doesn't require immediate responses. Just because something pops up on your screen doesn't mean you need to respond to it immediately. This one small distraction can really throw your day off track.

- Adam Braun, cofounder and CEO of MissionU, says, "I like to start my day with human contact—not digital contact." He went on to explain how he spend. the first part of his day meditating and with his wife and kids.
- Let friends, family, and colleagues know that sometimes you don't respond to texts right away. Give people a time frame for when they can plan to hear back from you (such as 24 hours) and stick with your plans.
- Keep response times consistent. If you always respond right away and then you suddenly stop, people are going to be confused. If you have a standing phone date for whatever reason, send people a note so they aren't worried about you if you don't call.
- Save all contacts, but don't keep random numbers or messages on your phone.
- Don't have long conversations or arguments over text! Tone in texts (like tone in e-mails) can be hard to interpret.
- Try to avoid a ton of back-and-forth via text. Always choose a two-minute chat over a one-hour text session.
- Limit texting and social during work hours.
- Utilize airplane mode to limit functionality.
- Put your phone down at dinner.
- Try not to look at your phone right before bed or first thing in the morning. It's nice to start your day the way you want to instead of the way your phone commands.

- Put your phone down while driving. No texting and driving, no excuses. Listen to your voice mails and keep them as close to zero as possible.
- Organize apps into categories (for example: travel, lifestyle, notebooks, business, shopping, etc.), delete those you haven't used in the past three months, and keep them updated.

## Quick Tips for Texting with Professional Contacts

- Only use emojis if the other person uses them first, especially if people are superior in role or title.
- Keep texts within reasonable hours (no early mornings, late nights, or weekends unless it's an emergency).
- Avoid acronyms such as LOL, ROFL, FOMO, etc.
- Always write in complete sentences.
- Remember to say "please" and "thank you."

# DISCONNECTION

The other night, my mom told me she was walking into a movie and her phone would be off. I said, "You know you can just turn the ringer off, right?"

"I like to turn it off," she responded.

The next day, I sat in a presentation for two hours, where my phone was on silent but certainly not off. This got me thinking, when is my phone ever off? The answer? Only when it dies.

My phone is *never* off. While I usually don't have the ringer on, it's still always on. We all seem to talk about disconnection and the importance of it—but we never actually shut off our phones. And why not? I mean, we can all say things like "Oh, I need it on me at all times for emergencies," but if we unpack that, it's probably a lie we've told ourselves. We're likely just concerned that if we don't see everything that happens on our phones, we might miss something. What would happen if we all shut our phones off for two hours each day, one during work and one while we are home? Give it a try one day this week. Keep track of what you accomplish when your phone is off. You might find you're more productive, or it may just lift some weight off your shoulders so you can relax.

## Bonus Tip

### Eliminate Screen Time

Ashley Robertson, founder of The Teacher Diva and content creator, says we should find ways to eliminate screen time. She and her husband are experimenting with turning their phone on grayscale, which makes everything on your phone black and white. The *New York Times* article "Is the Answer to Phone Addiction a Worse Phone?" explains that grayscale helps you disconnect from your phone because the lack of colors makes your phone less stimulating. (If you have an iPhone you can make this change by going to Settings > General > Accessibility > Display Accommodations > Color Filters. Turn Switch Color on and select Grayscale. The process differs for Android phones.)

# EXPERIMENT AND GROW

As you continue exploring the world of disconnection, you need to experiment and push further. First, think about any times of the day or week when you don't have access to your phone. For me, it's when I'm flying (although sometimes I'm on the Wi-Fi), in a workout class, working out with a trainer, sleeping, in the shower, watching a television show (sometimes), in a business meeting, or speaking to a class.

What about you? When do you disconnect? Write in below.

_____

Next, think about how you feel while you do those tasks. I know I feel productive, free, and relaxed. I'm free to concentrate on the moment and temporarily released from the daily pressures I face.

So, how do you feel when you disconnect? Fill in below.

_____

We all feel so trapped by our technology, like we can't escape it. But the truth is, we can. We control our social media platforms—they don't control us. But our actions must demonstrate that. If we let our phones control our lives, they will.

Each time you open an app, remember your reason for using it in the first place. Don't forget to regulate the time you are spending on apps each day, and catch yourself when you are using them for reasons other than what you've intended.

And finally, disconnect. Leave your phone home, shut it off or hide it across the room. Remember that you are in charge of you, not your devices. Part of getting our lives together is feeling like we own our time, and if our social networks own our time, we'll never feel like we've got it all together. So take back your time, and be intentional about it.

# *Chapter* 8

# MANAGE YOUR RELATIONSHIPS

Our relationships are everything. My professional relationships are the reason I am where I am today. Looking back, my very first job after college (at a talent agency) came to be because of a relationship I had cultivated during a previous summer internship experience. My first big brand deal with the Ford Motor Company became a reality thanks to a mentor I first interacted with on a cold call. That deal catapulted my business and changed it forever. And personal relationships are no different. These people make us feel important, loved, cared for, and more. If we didn't have amazing personal relationships, who would we call when we accomplish something big or make a huge mistake at work? Who would we call when we have a bad day or really good day?

I spoke on a panel at UCLA recently, and when executives were asked how they stay sane in today's chaotic world, everyone commented on the power of a support system. And they are right—with the right support system in place (at work and at home), you can do anything.

# PROFESSIONAL RELATIONSHIPS

In this section, we'll cover how to manage your relationship both inside and outside of the office. Let's get into it!

## Who Are Your Work People?

Let's start with an exercise to evaluate your work relationships. While the size of your team may be very different from mine, let's try to assess the relationships you have with the people you interact with the most day to day. This includes people you have both positive and negative relationships with. If there's someone in the office that you've been having trouble connecting with, evaluate that relationship here. I also encourage you to evaluate your relationship with your boss, mentors, and teammates. You can also look back at the communication log you created in Chapter 4 and include those relationships. The idea here is that we are examining specific relationships, looking at the reasons why each relationship is or is not working, and proactively coming up with solutions on how to enhance these workplace relationships. I made an example relationship assessment chart on the following page and included space for you to add your own relationships as well.

## LAUREN'S RELATIONSHIP CHART

| Relationship Type | Name of Person | Best Part of Relationship | Challenging Part of Relationship | Solution (Something YOU can do to make it better) |
|---|---|---|---|---|
| Boss | Meghan Maxey | Encouraging | Micro-Manager | Do a better job of communicating workload and managing "up" |
| Colleague | Sara Grossman | My work BFF | Sometimes people group us together and think we're the same person. Seriously. | Make sure I'm going out of my way to build my own relationships and express my own goals so that I'm not always grouped together with Sara. We aren't the same person. |
| Colleague | Rob Forman | I can't think of any. | Treats me poorly. | Find time to go to coffee outside of the office and discuss my problems and what we can do to fix them. Speak to team leader if it escalates. |
| Colleague | Ashley Silbermann | Strong Work Ethic | Slightly annoying and "too excited" | Try to set some boundaries and create check-in times |

## MY RELATIONSHIP CHART

| Relationship Type | Name of Person | Best Part of Relationship | Challenging Part of Relationship | Solution (Something YOU can do to make it better) |
|---|---|---|---|---|
| | | | | |
| | | | | |
| | | | | |
| | | | | |

## Handle Conflict at Work Constructively

When CPP Inc., the publishers of the Myers-Briggs Assessment and the Thomas-Kilmann Conflict Mode Instrument, commissioned a study on workplace conflict, it found that US employees spent 2.8 hours per week dealing with conflict. This amounts to approximately $359 billion in paid hours.[1]

To get it together, you want to eliminate and avoid conflict personally or professionally. Many argue that conflict is unavoidable. Mike Myatt, a Forbes contributor, wrote in an article in 2012, "While you can try and avoid conflict . . . , you cannot escape conflict."[2] He goes on to say that conflict is coming for you, regardless of if you seek it out or not.

Remember group projects in school? There was always someone you liked and someone you didn't like that you had to work with. As long as you are flexible and adapt to what's going on around you while trying your best to work with the resources that you have, you will find success.

Here are 10 tips on how you can effectively handle conflict in the workplace:

1. **Avoid the drama.** Sure, gossip and drama at work sometimes makes the day go by faster, but it's not worth your involvement. No matter what, do whatever you can to avoid the drama. This is work, not high school.
2. **Be proactive and solution-oriented.** Always be looking for an answer to the question, "What can we do to work together more effectively?" Aim to constantly get ahead of the problem.

3. **Confront the situation.** Speak to your colleague directly about whatever is bothering you. You spend too much time at work—why make it more stressful?

4. **Cool heads prevail.** David W. Ballard, head of the American Psychological Association's Psychologically Healthy Workplace Program, says, "Address the issue early, before it turns into a bigger problem, but be sure to wait until things have cooled down. It's difficult to have a productive discussion if you and your coworker are angry or upset. Wait until you both are clear-headed." When you have a conflict at work, even the smallest issues, can seem like the end of the world. As Ballard suggests, take a moment to let things calm down before you attempt to discuss with a coworker.[3]

5. **Self-evaluate.** What role do you play in this issue? Determine how you can be more solution-oriented and help to better the situation, then act!

6. **Practice active listening.** When you speak to your colleagues, hear them out. Instead of coming at them with everything they've done wrong, take a moment to really hear what they have to say.

7. **Discuss away from others.** Don't try to work out problems inside the office unless you have privacy. Your neighbors don't need to hear your arguments.

8. **Don't talk to coworkers about it.** You can vent to family and friends, but leave people close to the situation out of it. If you start gossiping or picking sides in office drama, it will just create more chaos.

Impress your coworkers by addressing conflict head-on, not complaining or gossiping about the situation.

9. **Challenge yourself to fix the problem.** Don't let yourself sit in a bad mood. Instead, try to understand the other person's perspective and think of a productive solution.

10. **Alert human resources or your supervisor.** If you try everything in your power to fix an issue and have no luck, elevate the conversation to the next level. One way or another, this needs to get fixed. If you ever feel uncomfortable or unsafe, go to human resources or your supervisor immediately.

## Maintain Professional Relationships

Look, relationships aren't easy, but building them up and maintaining them in a positive manner is important. These relationships and people don't go away. Even if people leave your company, you may work with them at a future job. They could be responsible for hiring you at a future job—who knows! I've seen former interns go on to be future decision makers. Trust me, they always come back around.

## Stay in Touch

My rule has always been that you should stay in touch with professional contacts by speaking with each person at least three times per year. Whether this is something organic or planned, it's important to maintain a strong network.

If something comes up that makes you think of contacts, let them know! Quick "thinking of you" texts, e-mails, or messages are easy ways to stay in touch and say hello without demanding some sort of major time-consuming response back.

While these organic situations are ideal, it's still important for you to reach out to every contact one time in the fall, summer, and spring. Doing this ensures that you stay relevant and top of mind to the people in your network. Plus, asking for a favor when a need comes up won't be awkward because you've been in touch frequently.

How do I actually make this happen? Here are my three tips:

1. Put a reminder on your calendar. I set reminders at the top of my calendar in January (usually the second week of the calendar year), early June, and late October to check in with my professional contacts. This covers my spring, summer, and fall reach outs! This is how I remember that it's time to do the rounds!

2. I have an Outlook folder named "Contacts." Anytime I'm e-mailing with people who aren't a cold pitch, client, or friend, I put their e-mail in the Contacts folder. Three times a year, I go into this folder and message everyone. It usually takes me a few hours a day for a week to get through everyone. What I've found over the time is that the stronger the relationships become, the more frequently you end up speaking with people organically. I find that I'm

constantly surprised by how many people I've already been in touch with when I check this folder every few months.

3. I usually create a short e-mail template that I can personalize and send to each contact. For example, my template could be "I just wanted to touch base and say hello. Hope all is well. I've been busy working on my third book—and thought of you! All my best to the team." But my personalized e-mail to my former internship coordinator (who is friends with Will Farrell) might say: "Hi Eric! I just wanted to touch base and say hello. Hope all is well. I've been busy working on my third book—and thought of you! Funny enough, we saw *Dear Evan Hansen* last week, and Will Farrell sat right behind us—Ha! All my best to you and your family!"

## Keep up with News About Your Contacts

Utilize tools like LinkedIn to keep up with professional news about your contacts. Doing this means you will have relevant information and lots to say when you reach out to say hello!

## The Birthday Phone Call

Remember people's birthdays! Everyone loves receiving birthday cards and phone calls on their special day. This is an easy way to stay in touch and leverage professional relationships. Put these dates in your calendar as reoccurring events so you remember from year to year.

## ...ink Ahead and Send Thoughtful Gifts

y first boss used to have me keep a file of gift ideas for her
..ients. She would hand me magazine cutouts or send me
..nks so that she always had gift ideas handy. This was a great
..ay to avoid wasting time and eliminate stress because she
..lready had ideas ready to go when it was time for another
..irthday!

I'd recommend creating a folder or file like this for yourself
..nd storing great gift ideas there. Whenever you screenshot
..omething cute on Instagram or find a creative idea on Etsy,
..-mail it to yourself and save it in this folder. Another gift-
..elated idea is to challenge yourself to buy your gifts the first
..week of each quarter. For example, here's a list of everything
..I need to buy a gift for in the second quarter:

- My husband's birthday (which is the same as mine—
  fun fact!)
- My friend Rob's birthday (A few friends and I usually
  split his gift, so I'm already getting this conversation
  started.)
- My brother's birthday
- My almost sister-in-law's bachelorette party
- My friend Samantha's and her son's birthdays

The first week of the quarter, I block out a few nights for either
mall or online shopping. I make a big list of all the upcoming
birthdays, babies, and events that are coming and buy everything at once.

If this doesn't seem feasible for you because you can't
afford gifts for each and every birthday, sending a card or

a recent photo you took together is a kind gesture that go
a long way. It's not about the money. I challenge you to a:
yourself, "What small gesture can I make to acknowledg
these people's birthdays and make them feel special?"

## Thank You Notes

While we briefly touched on thank you notes for mentors in .
previous chapter, the power of a thank you note is too big t
only discuss once!

Thank you notes are a great way to build a relationshir
with others. Go to the store, grab a pack of blank thank you
cards, and you will be ready to go. If you want to get fancy,
you can invest in some personalized cards with your name or
initials on the front. If someone gets you a gift, does something nice for you, or is just a pleasure to work with, send the
person a thank you note. As an internship and career expert,
I'm always talking about the power and value of a thank you
note. Lately, I've been challenging myself to write two thank
you notes each week. This week I wrote two thank you cards
to Kohl's executives I met in NYC who took care of me while
I spoke at a conference. If you had to write one or two thank
you notes per week, to whom would you send them?

I put a reminder in my calendar to do this. It's an easy way
to spend five minutes and go the extra mile. I challenge you
to put a weekly calendar reminder on a specific day for yourself. Block out 30 minutes to write two thank you notes and
send them out.

Whom will you send your first two thank you cards to?
Write their names here:

_____

_____

# PERSONAL RELATIONSHIPS

My friends and family give me confidence. They are like my own personal army, bodyguards, and protectors. They tell me the truth about everything (sometimes too much truth), but should I ever get hurt, they are the people who will undoubtedly have my back.

While the focus of this book is the workplace, personal relationships are a crucial part of all of our lives. I don't know about you, but if I'm in an argument with a family member or friend, I'm 100 percent distracted during the workday. Sometimes managing personal relationships can feel like a second job, and that's probably because relationships require work. But, in order to get it together, we must better manage our personal relationships and focus on them just as much (if not more) than our work relationships.

The following pages contain my personal strategies for managing and maintaining strong personal relationships.

## Who Are Your Life People?

Figuring out who are the most important people in your life is the first step in maintaining the right personal relationships. When determining those I want to prioritize in my life, I like to ask myself these questions:

- Whom could you call to take you to the hospital if you were sick?
- Who would take you to the airport if you needed a rid
- Who always has your back?
- Who gets upset when others treat you poorly?
- Who would be the president of your fan club?
- Who gives you constructive criticism because they want you to be the best you?
- Who makes you feel confident?
- Who would ride with you in the car for no reason other than to be around you?
- When you see this definition of *love*, who does it make you think of: "love is an intense feeling of deep affection"?

When I interviewed Adam Braun, I wanted to ask him about personal relationships. Knowing that his brother is Scooter Braun (the famous manager of Justin Bieber and other pop stars), I was curious as to how that affected his relationships. How did he avoid getting wrapped up in the world of Hollywood and the seemingly cool circles that surround his family?

Adam candidly told me that once he got married and had children, all of it faded away and became irrelevant. He said he stopped thinking about all of that and adopted this mentality: "I identify relationships that are going to be enriching, where I can bring value to their life and vice versa. What matters most to me is authenticity—my friendships aren't built on what's cool and what's not cool."

With all of this in mind, who are the friends and family you want to maintain strong relationships with? Write down ur quick list here (I recommend including at least five to ght people):

_____

_____

_____

_____

_____

_____

_____

_____

In Chapter 4, I talked about the communication log in your bullet journal and encouraged you to put the people that you want to stay in touch with frequently on that list. I assume that most of those people are going to be on your list above as well. For me, there are about five to eight people whom I like to be in touch with on a weekly (if not daily) basis. If there are any missing names on your communication log from Chapter 2, add them there now.

## Dealing with Friend Arguments

I know we've all been stuck in the middle of a big friend fight before. Trying to get work done while aggressive texts are coming in on the group text chain is nearly impossible. These are your favorite people, and you don't want to be arguing with them. But what can you do to proactively help the situation? Here are some thoughts: vent outside the group (to not chat members), reassure your friends that they aren't going to lose anyone over this discussion, and maintain individual relationships within groups.

It's also to important to remember that while we do tend to gravitate toward people who are like us, we are not exact clones of one another. We all perceive things differently and send messages differently. Getting it together means understanding that you can't control people (even the people you love), and you can't force people to do certain things or make certain decisions.

## Creating Boundaries

Last week, I called my brother and his fiancée at about 8:30 p.m. my time/11:30 p.m. their time (they are usually awake this late) to chat about nothing, as usual. When my brother picked up, he said, "Hey, think you could call us any earlier? These super late calls are difficult." At the time, I thought it was a funny but fair complaint, but the longer I sat there and thought about the importance of creating boundaries, the more I realized he may have been trying to create one for me.

Based on our discussion, it sounded like he and his fiancée were trying to get to sleep earlier and find time to relax before bed. My phone calls right before their heads hit the pillow likely weren't the most relaxing thing in the world.

That phone call and my brother's response taught me something really important that day that I haven't been able to stop thinking about since: you cannot live the life you ant and achieve your goals without setting some sort of oundaries.

## Communicate Boundaries

While deciding on a boundary is a great first step in creating a schedule that works for you, you can't just create the boundary in your head. You need to make people aware of it too.

For me, when I'm in writing mode and need every second to get writing done, I know I'm not going to answer the phone when friends call. So letting them know this ahead of time will be an effective way for me to set boundaries.

I also believe that because people and your relationships are sensitive, doing what you can to keep all parties happy is important. When setting a boundary, communicate how much you enjoy speaking with the other person and let him or her know you're looking forward to your next chat. If the boundary comes across as "I don't care about you," feelings could get hurt.

## The Power of No

I'm good at spending *my* time in the way *others* want to spend it. Let's look at an example of something that happened to me recently. A friend of mine wanted to go to Scottsdale for the weekend. Without thinking much about it, I said yes. Another friend wanted to go on a wine tasting overnight a few days later, and I also said yes. Another friend wanted to wake up at 7 a.m. the day after for a hike, and I said yes once again. While all these things are fun, having so many things

to do in such a short amount of time may not be in line wit
how I want to spend my time.

I'm often too quick to commit to others and too late t
realize that I have overcommitted, resulting in yet anothe
jam-packed weekend with not a second to spare for myself.

Challenge yourself to restrain from quick commitment
like this before you get to the inevitable tipping point.

My husband and I both run our own businesses and have
*very* flexible schedules. We are people who can be everywhere,
go to everything, and celebrate with everyone. But trust me,
once you do that for long enough, you get tired and the fun
times start to feel like work. It's all about finding that balance
and taking back control of your time and how you spend it.

## Other Quick Ways to Stay in Touch

While some of these have already been talked about, it's
important to remember all of the ways you can stay in touch
with friends. I use these on a regular basis!

- **Car catch-ups.** Before I get in the car, I go through my
  communication list of friends to make sure I'm doing
  my part to stay in touch. If not, I call them (hands-
  free) in the car to make the most of my time.
- **Social media.** I use social media to stay on top of
  what my friends are up to. I'll check out the photos of
  their kids and their status updates, and comment on
  their stuff.
- **Group text chats.** While these can be overwhelming,
  it's nice to communicate with everyone in one place.

- **Quick chats.** I try to speak to friends frequently so that we don't need to have hourlong catch-up conversations. It's tricky to find time for that.
- **Celebrate from afar.** No matter how far away you are, celebrate with your friends and family. I celebrate with my friends from Florida by calling and singing to them on their birthdays, and sometimes I send gifts.
- **Making plans.** I try to see my friends and family who live in other states at least once or twice per year, and those in the same city at least a few times per month. We all get wrapped up in our busy schedules and workload, but at some point, we have to prioritize our relationships and figure it out.
- **Make a standing plan.** Invite friends to things you like to attend regularly on your own time. For example, if you hike every Saturday, invite friends to join!
- **Weekend work parties.** Sometimes my friends and I will have "weekend work parties" at coffee shops around town where we all bring our computers and work on whatever we need to get done. This kills two birds with one stone: productivity time and time with friends.
- **Planning ahead.** Look at your schedule ahead of time to identify opportunities for making plans. If you're traveling where you know a friend lives, reach out in advance to meet up.
- **Let people know you are thinking of them.** I mentioned this previously in the professional relationships section, but this tip can be useful with

personal friends as well. Think of fun ways to say, "I love and miss you," and it won't go unnoticed.

- **When things happen, pick up the phone.** When things happen to friends (good, bad, happy, sad), stop texting and pick up the phone. It's nice for them to hear the sincerity in your voice.

- **Ask for help.** If you are having a tough time, ask friends for help or advice. Don't be afraid to tell your closest friends that you are having a tough time.

- **Busy isn't an excuse.** If your personal relationships are your priority, then your actions need to match that. You can't always tell your closest people that you are too busy for them. Find a way to make it work.

- **Remember, plans change.** I'd try not to get *so* wrapped up in the plans that if they fall through for some reason, it's not the complete end of the world. And don't take it personally. Things happen.

• • •

Don't take your professional or personal relationships for granted. These are the people we go through life with, we face challenges with, we experience new things with. We need to value these relationships, take care of them, and be intentional with the way we handle them. To get our lives together, we need to prioritize these relationships, take the time to understand them, and make an intentional decision on how to handle them.

# Chapter 9

# PERSONAL WELLNESS

Working out, feeling like I'm in a positive mental state, keeping healthy, sleeping, and (most important) relaxing have been key in getting it together. Prioritizing personal wellness is something I'm ashamed to admit I didn't take seriously until this year. And sometimes it's difficult, because it means planning, sacrificing, and choosing the long-term result over the desire of the moment (like eating the big piece of chocolate cake in front of me).

Before this year, I spent more time thinking about work and people-pleasing than paying attention to my own personal wellness, and looking back, I think I suffered because of it. Since there's so much information to cover in this section, I've divided it into four sections: mental health, diet and exercise, power sleeping, and relaxation.

## MENTAL HEALTH

Merriam-Webster defines *mental health* as "the general condition of one's mental and emotional state." Mental health may include an individual's ability to enjoy life and create a balance between life activities and efforts.

I like to look at mental health as a goal. We all want to be satisfied with ourselves, enjoy life, and most important, create balance. But, in a world full of distraction, confusion, jealousy, and anger, how do we stay mentally strong?

Here are some of the ways you can master your mental health:

- **Get help.** Approximately one in five adults in the United States experience mental illness each year.[1] That number is jaw-dropping. First and foremost, if you are constantly battling negative thoughts, depression, or anxiety, please seek help from a trained medical professional. Therapists, psychiatrics, and psychologists are available and will give you the proper tools you need. Don't wait. Get help right away.
- **Give yourself pep talks.** I can't stress the importance of self-encouragement and positive reinforcement enough. Be nice to yourself, take care of yourself, and put yourself and your needs first. Tell yourself you did a great job today. Be proud of everything you've accomplished. Smile and remind yourself that you're a good person, son or daughter, parent, husband or wife, employee, boss, and friend.
- **Identify feelings and call them out.** We've all felt down before, it's inevitable. But if you begin to pay attention to when or why you feel this way, you'll begin to recognize similarities. Take the time to think about what you are feeling as well as when and why

you are feeling it. Not only will this be effective in the future, but it will also serve as a reminder that you've been here before and you can and will get through this.

- **Name the cause.** What is causing this instance? Say it aloud. Once I identify the cause, I remind myself that I am in control of my feelings. Then I examine my own actions and identify what got me to where I am.

- **Focus on accomplishments.** As I mentioned earlier, accomplishing something makes me feel better when I'm down. Figure out what makes you feel accomplished and do it!

- **Remind yourself of what makes you happy.** Remember the happiness page in your bullet journal? Use that list to refresh your memory and do something that you already know you enjoy.

- **Regulate social media.** We just had an entire chapter about social media, but I want to reiterate that if you don't watch how you spend your time on social, it can become an unhealthy habit.

- **Meditate.** Meditation was certainly a common theme among the experts that I interviewed. Adam Braun says he's been meditating for 13 years, and he says that when he doesn't practice meditation consistently, he doesn't feel peaceful. He explains, "Everything just feels too rushed." For beginners who want to start meditating, he recommends the apps Headspace, Calm, and Oak.

- **Get to know yourself better.** Identify what helps you relax, what motivates you, and what makes you feel better. At the end of this chapter, I call out 40 differen ways that you can relax and even encourage you to start your own list to turn to at any time.

- **Consult someone with similar experience.**
Speaking to other people in similar situations is a great way to feel heard and to find a productive solution to a problem you're facing. For example, if you're experiencing depression and know that family members have dealt with the same thing, give them a call. Talk with them about their journey, experiences, and resources. Remember, you are never alone.

• • •

Today, phrases including "meltdown," "panic attack," "anxious," and "stressed" are being used more and more to describe how we are feeling. We experience this because we don't have it together, and when you're running a hundred miles a minute in every different direction, how can you?

By changing the way we look at our struggles and focusing on the positive solutions instead of the negative feelings we are experiencing, we will walk away happier, healthier, and more effective in our work and relationships.

# DIET AND EXERCISE

We all have different reasons to take care of our bodies and maintain our physical health. No matter your reason, your ɔdy is your most important tool. If it's not in the best shape ossible, you're not going to be able to perform at your best in ll parts of your life.

So, how can we fine-tune our bodies and take care of ourelves to get the best results and performance possible?

The answer is twofold:

1. Take fitness seriously.
2. Eat clean.

And to clarify, you can't do one without the other. To maximize results, you must focus on both.

## Where Do You Fall?

Let's begin by determining where you are with our physical health right now.

On a scale of 1 to 10, how physically fit are you? To help with the scale, I'd say that if you work out religiously five to seven days a week and feel very confident about your strength and abilities, you are probably a 10. When I interviewed Laura Vanderkam (author of *Off the Clock*), she said she runs seven days a week, no matter what. I'd rank Laura a 10 on the physically fit level. If you never work out, it's not a focus or a priority; I'd rank yourself at a 1.

So, where do you fit on the scale?

• • •

Next, let's look at eating clean. To rank yourself a 10 in the eating category, you eat clean every single meal of the day, every day of the week (with a possible small exception here and there). If you are a 1, most of your meals aren't healthy—probably the opposite of healthy.

Where do you fall on the scale?

## Setting Reasonable Goals

Now that we know where we are, we need to establish some reasonable goals. My recommendation is to increase your ranking for both clean eating and physical fitness by two points. Once we decide where we are and where we need to be, we need a three-step Action Plan (see Chapter 4). Here is my three-step Action Plan for each of the categories (and I even included room for you to design your own plan).

---

**Lauren's Physical Fitness Action Plan**

- Work out with trainer at the gym two days per week.
- Go to the gym on my own to work out or take a class an additional two days per week.
- Do at least one active thing on the weekend.

---

**My Physical Fitness Action Plan**

- _____
- _____
- _____

## Lauren's Eating Clean Action Plan

- Control the meals I can.
- Focus on protein. I usually have some sort of protein with every meal, but the advice from my trainer was really to focus on the protein—it should be the "hero product" of every meal.
- Plan. For me, that means thinking about my meals ahead of time and planning accordingly.

## My Eating Clean Action Plan

- _____
- _____
- _____

All right, so we've reviewed where you are, where you want to be, and your plan for how to get there. Write these Action Plans in your bullet journal so you have everything in one place. For me, planning is usually the easy part and, frankly, the part I enjoy the most. Actually implementing and consistently following through with the plan is where I have trouble. The number one reason I didn't get to the gym in the past wasn't because of work, friends, my husband, or even time—it was *me*. One of the biggest challenges when it came to working out was taking myself seriously, not settling for my own excuses, and learning how to push myself (something that I'm still in the process of learning).

## Exercise

Here are some tips that have helped me workout consistentl

- **Get more sleep.** Later in this chapter, I'll talk about sleep habits and the power of good rest. If you're planning a morning workout, get to bed early enough that you don't feel stressed or tired.
- **Plan ahead.** Plan when you will be going to the gym or a class and put it in your calendar. When I interviewed Lauryn Hock (www.lauryncakes.com), she said she finds that when she puts exercise in her calendar appointment, she's more likely to go!
- **Pack your gym bag the night before.** Or, better yet, pack it on a Sunday for the entire week. I always pack as many outfits as days I plan to go to the gym that week. I also include one or two pairs of sneakers, my headphones, and extra hair ties. If you live in a city where you commute to work without a car, I recommend laying out four or five sets of gym clothes on Monday. Put them somewhere you can easily switch out your work clothes with a clean set of gym clothes for the following day.
- **Charge headphones!** I can't go to the gym without my headphones, so I always make sure they are ready to go in the morning. It's helpful to put your bag near these headphones so you can pick them both up when you leave.
- **Have a water bottle ready.** Make sure you have water ready to go in the refrigerator the night before. Or, treat yourself to an insulated water bottle that keeps

your drinks cold overnight so you have one less thing to remember in the morning.

- **Use apps when you can't get to the gym.** Sarah Boyd, founder of Simply, says she uses the Sweat App for a 28-minute workout in the morning before heading into the office. We all have days when we can't get to the gym for one reason or another, so using an app (personal favorites include Studio Tone It Up or Body Love by Anna Victoria) makes quick workouts at home possible.

- **Don't break the streak.** Try to keep up your gym routine because once you break it, it's always harder to go back. Even when you travel. Use the hotel fitness center, a gym you are a part of, or try a class nearby. Whatever you do, keep up with your workouts!

- **Go to classes.** The nice thing about classes is that you keep moving because the class is moving. When I'm with the trainer one-on-one, it's easier for me to stop and chitchat. I always work up a sweat in a gym class.

- **Ask questions at the gym.** Take advantage of the trainers at the gym, especially the free intro sessions that you get when you join a new gym. Ask questions about what your daily routine should look like. Even if you work out with a trainer (as I do), I'm always asking him questions so that when I come to the gym alone (or any other gym in the country), I know what to do with the equipment.

- **Challenge yourself and switch it up.** What can you do today that is a little bit harder than yesterday? Challenge yourself and keep things fun by switching it up. OUR bodies get used to routines, so doing the same workouts or classes every day may get stale.

- **Emphasize stretching.** Make sure to stretch at the beginning and end of your workouts. Ask your trainer at your local gym to help guide you through proper stretches and how you can use the foam rollers (my favorite!) the right way.

- **Weigh in and measure frequently.** Weighing in all the time can be frustrating, so I suggest tracking your measurements, too. Check your progress as it makes sense for you.

- **Morning pep talk.** I like to remind myself of my goals in the morning and ask myself, "What's one thing you can do today to hit your fitness goal?" It may be small that day, but I pick one thing and make sure to do at least that.

- **Tell friends your goals.** Often friends get competitive about goals and losing weight, but this is unnecessary. My solution? Be honest and up front with your friends about your personal goals. Usually, it's easier to make people feel like they are included in your journey instead of on the outside of it.

- **Log calories.** I use MyFitnessPal (the free version) to log calories, or I write down what I eat on my iPhone notepad to review with my trainer while we're working out. When you take the time to write down what you eat, you start noticing patterns you might not otherwise see.

- **Food accountability group.** My friend Rachel (CEO and founder of GlamourGals) was in town the other night, and at dinner, she kept taking photos of her food. She showed me how she and a handful of friends were in a chat group on WhatsApp called Food Group, and they would show everything they ate to one another. The goal of the group was to be aware of what they were eating, choose healthy options, and get inspired by their friends' healthy choices.

## How to Look Put Together for Work, Post-Gym

Congrats! You got up early (pre-work) to go to the gym. But now you must get ready—and fast! Here are my tips to look acceptable at work quickly:

- I do my hair the night before.
- I pack an easy outfit.
- I pack shower essentials (including towels).
- I bring my makeup bag.
- I don't forget work shoes.

When I am done working out, I dive right into the shower at the gym and give myself a max of five minutes each to get my hair and makeup done. If I can jump into my clothes quickly, I'm out of there in less than 20 minutes. I usually have a busy day ahead and can still stop at Starbucks on the way in!

## Diet

Working out consistently is part of getting it together, but eating healthy is crucial if you want to see results. My eating habits have varied over the years, and now I strive for clean eating whenever I can control it—because there are certainly times when I want (and deserve) to treat myself!

I have a few tips that should help get you on your way:

- **Don't let friends throw you off.** Just like you shouldn't be scared to tell your friends about your fitness goals, you shouldn't be scared to tell them that you're interested in eating lighter and healthier too. They are your friends, so they will respect you.
- **Remind yourself of your reason.** What's your reason for working out? Remember, you should be able to say it loud and be proud.
- **Grocery shopping.** It all starts at the store with healthy purchasing habits. Contrary to popular belief, you don't have to spend all your money to eat healthy. Focus on proteins for lunches and dinners and food prep. What can you cook and prep on a Sunday night so you can eat it for the rest of the week? Go crazy in the fresh produce section.

## My Favorite Healthy Snacks

At Intern Queen, we made a YouTube video covering our team's favorite snacks at work. Of course, I wanted to highlight healthy snacks and had to remove the Flamin' Hot Cheetos from the list! Here's our list of favorite healthy snacks:

- Veggie sticks
- Carrots and hummus
- Rice cakes and peanut butter
- Roasted seaweed
- Granola bars (pick your favorite kinds)
- Fig bars!
- Sliced apples
- Trail mix (watch out for the ones with chocolate chips!)
- Nuts
- Precut fruit
- Berries
- Protein bars
- Purse snacks

---

- **Drink enough water.** Right before I started writing this book, one of my closest friends gave me a hard-core lecture (in public) about how I need to drink more water. And she was right, because the benefits of drinking water include clearer skin, boosts in productivity, decreased fatigue, and much more. Find a cup or bottle that you can use for water every day, and start taking it with you everywhere.
- **Don't go overboard.** You aren't going to be able to eat healthy every single meal of your life, and if you take it to an extreme level, you may be setting yourself up for disappointment. Give yourself a break every so often.
- **Consider the substitutes.** In today's world, there is a substitute for almost everything. Instead of eggs, get

egg whites. Instead of coffee creamer, get almond milk. Instead of pizza crust, there's cauliflower crust. The list goes on. I'm not standing by any of these substitutes, but understand your options and experiment.

- **Plan ahead.** I know we talk about planning ahead and preparation so much in this book, but it's imperative when it comes to getting it together. If you know that pizza night is coming up, prep for it by eating healthy in the days leading up to it.
- **Meal prep.** I haven't always been a fan of meal prepping. I didn't understand why I should go through the trouble of prepping so much food. Our interns inspired me to give it a try. They explained that having meals ready to go saved them money and time, was a guarantee the meal was healthy, and makes the process of dealing with dietary restrictions easier. With so many positives, it was hard to ignore. This is now part of my routine!

• • •

Self-evaluation is crucial when it comes to working out and trying to eat healthy. If something isn't working, change it up. Keep asking yourself questions, and keep a tight watch.

# SLEEP *IS* PART OF IT

I'm not a sleep expert and I don't always sleep as much as I should, but I have realized (quite recently) that to get it together, I needed to get more sleep. I was both shocked and frightened when I read in her book *Thrive* that Ariana Huffington (whom I *so* admire) collapsed in 2007 due to lack of sleep. Honestly, I didn't know that was possible! Ariana explains, "Often the first things we give up are those that nourish us the most but seem optional." Ariana's words are true to many, including myself. We tend to convince ourselves that getting enough sleep is optional, but this is a huge oversight that we need to address!

I mean, here we are, complaining about how we can't seem to get it together, yet we all have a solution right in front of us: sleep!

The benefits of getting enough sleep are astounding. By getting the necessary seven to eight hours of sleep you need, you will see positive shifts in mood, improved relationships, higher quality work, lower levels of stress, weight maintenance and loss,[2] as well as an increase in memory, performance, creativity, and much more.[3] With a list of benefits this long, how can we afford not to prioritize sleep? I know it inspired me to make a change.

## How I Changed My Sleep Habits

It was a Sunday in March, and I had made plans to wake up early on Monday and go to the gym before work. I was excited to wake up and start my day off feeling strong.

Nighttime arrived, and per usual, I stayed up late preparing for the next day in the office. I finally shut my computer and got into bed around midnight and just couldn't fall asleep. I turned on the TV to watch a show, and by the time the episode was over, it was after 1 a.m. I looked at the clock and did the math. I growled under my breath, "Even if I fall asleep in the next 15 minutes (which doesn't feel likely), I'd still get less than five hours of sleep." I laid there, stressing about the next morning, mad at myself for making the goal in the first place. I finally dozed off at some point, but when I woke up the next morning, I had absolutely no desire to follow through with my workout. What was wrong with me?

I was going to bed too late to allow myself the proper time to rest and recharge for the next day. But, that wasn't my only issue. I also wasn't wrapping up my night early enough. I knew I needed two things: a longer transition time between working and sleeping and to get into bed earlier. I wanted to figure out exactly how long I needed to make both things happen, so I put my body to the test.

The first night I started my experiment, I stopped working at 9 p.m. I wanted to see how long it would take me to fall asleep. I wasn't tired at all, so I looked for activities to make me feel relaxed and ready for bed. I took a hot shower, painted on a charcoal face mask, scrolled the shopping sites on my phone, looked up celebrities on Instagram, and watched hours of TV. No matter what I did, I still wasn't tired. Finally, at 11 p.m., I poured myself half a glass of red wine ("sleepy juice" as I like to call it), and that did the trick.

It took me about three hours to transition from *do* mode to *do nothing* mode. Looking back, it was a bit ridiculous to think my body could just seamlessly transition from go mode to sleep mode.

The next night, I tried a new method. I planned to work out in the morning, which required me to be up by 6 a.m.

I did some research and found that the National Sleep Foundation says that adults between the ages of 18 and 64 require seven to nine hours of sleep. So I planned accordingly.

In order to get seven to eight hours of sleep, I had to be asleep between 11 p.m. and 12 a.m. I intentionally wrapped up work by 8 p.m. and went upstairs to wind down for the night. My evening wind down routine consisted of the following:

1. Organizing my work clothes and gym bag for the next day
2. Showering with the lights off and a lit candle
3. Putting on a face mask while I cleaned my bedroom and some makeup brushes
4. Blowing out my hair for the next day
5. Watching clips of *The View* from earlier that day
6. Reading on my iBooks app
7. Watching one episode of a calm 30-minute show on Netflix (No *Homeland* before bed for me. It gets me too hyped up.)

I really enjoyed my evening routine as it felt like *me* time. Sure enough, it worked too. I fell asleep just after 11 p.m., woke up feeling refreshed at 6 a.m., and had a successful workout.

This new routine is now an important part of each day. Because I put getting a good night of sleep before everything else, I wake up feeling so much better than I did before. Instead of feeling groggy and that I need coffee to make it through the day, I feel energized and excited to get my day started.

• • •

When I interviewed Brooke Miccio for this book, one of the first things she said was, "Sleep is my priority. I am always aware of the time I'm going to bed. Last night, I was up late working on a project until about 2 a.m. Because of that, I let myself sleep in this morning. I'm always trying to make sure I get enough sleep." Brooke also stresses the importance of a "wind down" plan before she goes to bed. I asked her what her routine looked like and she said, "I shower at night and have a skin care routine with lotions and face masks." She said she loves to self-pamper and journal in bed.

Brooke also stresses the importance of turning off all devices an hour before bed, and the National Sleep Foundation has done research to prove this makes a significant difference in your sleep patterns. She also suggests putting your phone on night shift mode, which eliminates harmful blue light in our phones. In addition to negatively impacting your sleep patterns, studies show that this blue light may contribute to cancer, diabetes, heart disease, and obesity too.

Moving forward, disconnecting from technology (yes, even television) is a goal I continue to work toward as I get it together.

# RELAXING

An essential part of personal wellness is self-care. You must make time for yourself and prioritize relaxation.

Oftentimes, we are so busy trying to be and look our best that we forget we all need time to relax. Relaxation, done properly, is a crucial part of all our lives.

## Make Time for You

Looking at your daily schedule, do you see free time in your day? I want you to find three 20- to 60-minute timeslots each week and mark them as relax zones for yourself.

When I look at my weekly calendar, it can be hectic and filled with almost zero downtime. Since writing this book, I've changed, that and I now make it a priority to find time in each day for me.

Look, I know it's hard to find time for yourself, it really is. But we must shut up and figure it out. This may be blunt, but it's the truth. Once you find the time slots that you can own, you must determine how you want to spend this time. Here are 40 activities that help me feel more relaxed and give me more time in my day. I challenge you to start your own list of activities that you can turn to when you need to relax and take a well-deserved break. Start your own list in your new notebook and turn to it whenever you need some time for you!

### *My 40 Favorite Ways to Relax*

1. **Make two plans per weekend.** Don't overplan or let the "fear of missing out" (or FOMO) take over. Only commit to two things each weekend.

2. **Stop feeling weird about spending time alone.**
   One of my friends thinks that people who eat,
   travel, or go to movies or concerts alone are weird. I
   couldn't disagree more. We all need time alone—and
   you are great company!

3. **Become a tea person.** Making myself some hot tea
   in my huge mugs that say "Think" and "Pause" helps
   me relax and bring my day to an end.

4. **Embrace boredom.** A researcher from the
   University of Louisville explains that "boredom
   gives us the push to switch goals and projects." Being
   bored pushes us, so instead of fearing boredom,
   embrace it, I know I do.

5. **Track your happy.** As I suggested in Chapter 3,
   write down activities that make you happy so that
   when you are feeling bummed, you can replicate
   those ideas. In fact, once you try out some of the
   suggestions on this list, add them to your own
   happiness page.

6. **Go on walks.** Walking around the block with my
   husband without my phone is one of our favorite
   things to do each day. We unwind, chat about work,
   and enjoy some quality time together.

7. **Travel.** Making time for personal travel (even if it's
   so close you can drive) is a great way to experience
   and discover new things.

8. **Put on headphones.** I talked about my new
   headphones a few times, and no matter what, putting
   on my Beats helps me go into my own bubble.

9. **Morning workouts.** Working out first thing in the morning makes me feel like I started my day off on the right foot and allows me to go home right after work and relax.

10. **Castle day.** At least one or two times a month, I have what I call a castle day where I do nothing but hang out at home (aka my castle) and relax. You can clean up, accomplish tasks, catch up on sleep, or watch some of your favorite TV shows.

11. **Give yourself time to reflect.** Do you ever feel like you go through life with all of these cool plans, opportunities, and memories, but you are so busy rushing through them that you never have a chance to actually sit down and reflect? I used to feel that way frequently, but relaxing gives me the opportunity to reflect and stops my brain from saying "on to the next one."

12. **Mindless tasks.** Mindless tasks like laundry, cooking, or washing dishes help me unwind. There's something nice about attacking a project that you know you can complete easily.

13. **Journal.** "Free write" sessions allow you to work through what's working and what isn't, as well as identify successes, failures, and challenges you're facing.

14. **Say no.** If you don't want to do something, *just say no*. Practice setting healthy personal and professional boundaries so you can make time for and enjoy time alone.

15. **Treat yourself.** You deserve the little things that make you happy. Whether it's a walk during lunch, flowers at your desk, or piece of chocolate, treat yourself because you deserve it!

16. **Watch YouTube videos.** Videos clips from shows like Jimmy Fallon, Jimmy Kimmel, Ellen, and more always make me laugh—and who doesn't want to laugh more!

17. **Read.** Reading can be relaxing, fun, and informative. Whether you're reading a book, eBook, or magazine, this is a great way to spend time with you.

18. **Download a podcast.** Podcasts are great because you can listen to them anywhere. Whether you're on a plane or train or at home washing dishes, you can learn something new or listen to a fun discussion.

19. **Watch TV.** Whether it's a new, old, or reality TV show, I love binge-watching shows because it makes me feel relaxed and helps me escape the real world for a bit. *The West Wing*, *The Killing*, *The Good Wife*, and *Shameless* are some favorites to check out.

20. **Try something new!** Whether it's a new recipe, skill, or hobby, switch things up! YouTuber Michelle Phan told me she took an online calligraphy course because she wanted to try something different at night!

21. **Take a walk or go on a hike!** Going for a walk or hiking alone or with a friend can be fun. You'll get some exercise and be outside!

22. **Have a spa day.** These aren't a personal favorite for me, but so many others swear by them. Give it a try—plus, this is another treat yourself moment!

23. **Turn over your tech.** I talked about this during the social media and disconnection chapter (Chapter 7), but take an hour or two for yourself. If you can, take the day. Why do you need your phone, anyway?

24. **Apply a face mask.** There's something about sitting with a face mask on that makes me feel like I'm literally peeling off the day and the stresses that came with it. Right now, my favorites are by SheaMoisture and Origins.

25. **Turn your shower into a spa.** Have you ever been in the shower at a fancy spa? It's life-changing! Try to replicate this and make your shower a Zen zone!

26. **Create a nighttime routine.** Create your own routine that makes you feel relaxed. I look forward to coming home and following through with my routine.

27. **Plan a full day of fun.** Take your Saturday or Sunday back and plan something that has nothing to do with getting it together. Make it a day full of nothing but fun.

28. **Explore new music.** When the right song comes on and captures your mood, it can really transport you. Services like Apple Music, Spotify, and Pandora will introduce you to new music and artists.

29. **Shopping.** Shopping and looking at different outfits drives my creativity. I love walking around the mall

slowly with no place to be. Resisting sales might be hard, but this can be relaxing.

30. **Beach or pool.** Sitting on a lounge chair by the beach or pool feels like the ultimate form of relaxation for me. Just make sure you put on your sunscreen in case you fall asleep.

31. **Wear comfy clothes.** Everything is better in funny sweatpants and an old sweatshirt. If I'm lucky my hair is on top of my head and tied up with a big scrunchie. Now *that* is relaxation.

32. **Have a dance or singing party.** Sometimes relaxing can mean going out with friends to dance, laugh, sing, and have fun.

33. **Couching.** Looking back at the past year, some of my favorite times were sitting on the couch with my family members and my husband in sweats, talking, laughing, and being silly for hours.

34. **Bring on the nap.** There's nothing like taking a long nap in the middle of the day. Listen to when your body needs one, and it will be just the medicine you needed.

35. **Do some heavy sweating.** This isn't *my* cup of tea, but a new trend is sweat lodges (sort of like saunas) where you go and sweat for a short time period to release toxins and water weight.

36. **Enjoy the bubbles.** Take a bubble bath or drink some champagne. Either will work for some great relaxation.

37. **Meditate.** Studies show that meditation not only lowers stress levels but also decreases depression,

anxiety, pain, and insomnia. These same studies show that it can also increase your quality of life.[4] And so many successful people start their day with meditation including Ariana Huffington, Oprah, Jeff Winer (CEO of LinkedIn), Jerry Seinfeld, and Evan Williams (Twitter founder). They can't all be wrong!

38. **Attend a concert.** Opportunities to feel like a kid again can be fun and relaxing. Whatever you do, sing your heart out!

39. **Go outside.** Remember how you grew up outside? Get back out there. Throw the football around, go for a run, go do something outdoors. Get some fresh air!

40. **Play board games or cards.** If you want to play alone, solitaire or a crossword puzzle will do the trick. If you're with a group, bring out something you can all play together.

• • •

I love this chapter because it's not about work, social media, or other people. **It's about you**.

We spend so much of our daily lives focusing on other people, things, and commitments, but what about focusing on ourselves? I know this chapter includes a lot of information, but please take the time to consider it, absorb it, and maybe even try to live it a little. You can thank yourself later!

# NOTES

## Introduction

1. Laura Vanderkam, "The Busy Person's Lies," *New York Times*, May 13, 2016.
2. Erin Falconer, *How to Get Sh\*t Done* (New York: Simon & Schuster, 2018), 128.
3. Stress in America Survey, American Psychological Association website, August 2017.
4. http://www.simply-inc.com/.

## Chapter 1

1. Andreas Elpidorou, quoted in Vivian Giang, "The Science Behind How Boredom Benefits Creative Thought," FastCompany, February 9, 2015, https://www.fastcompany.com/3042046/the-science-behind-how -boredom-benefits-creative-thought.

## Chapter 3

1. Scott Petinga, "How to Embrace Failure in Order to Become Successful," Forbes.com, August 12, 2014, https://www.forbes.com/sites /theyec/2014/08/12/how-to-embrace-failure-in-order-to-become -successful/#5fb400531956.

2. Ryan Holiday, "Why You Should Embrace Failure," *Psychology Today*, May 12, 2014, https://www.psychologytoday.com/us/blog/the-obstacle -is-the-way/201405/why-you-should-embrace-failure.

3. Holiday, "Why You Should Embrace Failure."

## Chapter 4

1. Robert S. Rubin, "Will the Real SMART Goals Please Stand Up?," *The Industrial-Organizational Psychologist* 39, no. 4 (April 2002): 26–27.

## Chapter 5

1. John P. Robinson, "Americans Less Rushed but No Happier: 1965–2010 Trends in Subjective Time and Happiness," *Social Indicators Research* 113, no. 3 (September 2013): 1091–1104 (first online November 8, 2012).

## Chapter 6

1. Kat Boogaard, "Take It from Someone Who Hates Productivity Hacks—the Pomodoro Technique Actually Works," TheMuse.com, 2018.

## Chapter 7

1. Mediakix Team, "How Much Time Do We Spend on Social Media?," Mediakix, December 15, 2016, http://mediakix.com/2016/12/how -much-time-is-spent-on-social-media-lifetime/#gs.GClQVDQ.

## Chapter 8

1. Jennifer Lawler, "The Real Cost of Workplace Conflict," Entrepreneur.com, June 21, 2010.

2. Mike Myatt, "5 Keys of Dealing with Workplace Conflict," Forbes.com, February 22, 2012.

3. Jessica Harper, "10 Tips for Tackling the Toughest Workplace Conflicts," *US News*, July 18, 2012.

## Chapter 9

1. "Mental Illness," National Institute of Mental Health, accessed May 2, 2018, http://www.nimh.nih.gov/health/statistics/prevalence/any-mental-illness-ami-among-adults.shtml.

2. Esther Crain, "11 Biggest Health Benefits of Sleep," HuffPost, January 28, 2015, https://www.huffingtonpost.com/2015/01/28/biggest-sleep-health-bene_n_6549830.html.

3. Alyssa Sparacino, "11 Surprising Health Benefits of Sleep," Health.com, March 4, 2018, https://www.health.com/health/gallery/0,,20459221,00.html.

4. Brigid Schulte, "Harvard Neuroscientist: Meditation Not Only Reduces Stress, Here's How It Changes Your Brain," *Washington Post*, May 26, 2015, https://www.washingtonpost.com/news/inspired-life/wp/2015/05/26/harvard-neuroscientist-meditation-not-only-reduces-stress-it-literally-changes-your-brain/?utm_term=.9ccd093bd5da.

# INDEX

distraction-free work zone for,
119–120
efficient meetings for, 138–139
and finding your focus,
121–127
and holding yourself
accountable, 130–131
from home, 145–147
and learning, 136–137
networking for, 140–144
and prioritizing, 127–130
and receiving feedback,
144–145
and removing inefficiencies,
135–136
on the road, 148–151
and talk vs. action, 130
and thanking others, 137
using PDDs for, 134–135
and working up vs. working
out, 131–132
Gifts, sending, 179–180
GlamourGals, 10, 63, 123, 137,
198
Gmail, 102, 106
Goal list (Bullet Journal), 110
Goals, 71–96
biweekly, 80–81
and creating a Time Chart,
92–95
and creating an Action Plan,
82–91
determining your, 20
monthly, 78–81
for personal wellness, 198

quarterly, 76–81
restating, in Bullet Journal,
110
setting your, 73–74
SMART, 71–74
yearly, 76–78
YQMB, 74–85
Good stuff, celebrating the, 24
Google Calendar, 98
Google Docs, 115, 117
Google Drive, 117
Grayscale mode, 168
Grocery shopping, 200
Group text chats, 186
Gym bags, 196
Gym workouts, 196–198

Hadid, Gigi, 1
Haircuts, 151
Happiness page (Bullet Journal),
113, 191, 208
Headphones, 123, 196, 208
Headspace, 191
Health, evaluating your, 193
(see also Personal wellness)
Healthy boundaries, creating,
16–17, 124
Help:
asking for, 188
getting, 190
Hiking, 210
Hobbies, 210
Hock, Lauryn, 10–11, 41, 196
Holiday, Ryan, 58, 60, 61
Home, working from, 145–147

# ABOUT THE AUTHOR

**Lauren Berger** is CEO & Founder of both CareerQueen.com and InternQueen.com, together they reach over 6 million people and connect them with their dream careers. Berger has been a featured keynote at 200+ colleges, universities, leadership conferences, and entrepreneurship events. Her previous titles include the best-selling *All Work, No Pay* and *Welcome to*  *the Real World*. Berger's Youtube Channel, has over 1.2 million views and releases new content every Wednesday. Her Instagram, Twitter, Facebook, and LinkedIn reach over 100,000 people. Berger's career advice has been featured on The Today Show, KTLA, Fox & Friends, *Marie Claire*, WhoWhatWear, *Refinery29*, Entrepreneur on Fire, *Bustle*, CNBC, *Entrepreneur*, *Glamour*, and more. Berger not only delivers unique career advice to her audience, but also serves as a marketing agency that helps leading brands activate brand ambassadors and establish a presence with both college students and young professionals worldwide. Berger's business has doubled in recent years and her current roster of clients includes Michael Kors, Keurig, Whole Foods, Schwinn, Duncan Hines, Estee Lauder, and over 30 other top-notch brands.